NEW PENTECOST OR NEW PASSION?

New Pentecost

or

New Passion?

The Direction of Religious Life Today

Thomas E. Clarke, S.J.

PAULIST PRESS
Paramus / New York / Toronto

ACKNOWLEDGMENTS

Chapters 1, 6 and 8 originally appeared in *America*, in the editions of March 6, 1971, February 20, 1971, and April 19, 1969 respectively. Copyright © America Press Inc., 106 West 56th St., N.Y., N.Y. 10019. All rights reserved. Reprinted with permission. Chapters 2, 3 and 7 originally appeared in *The Way*, in the editions of April 1970, July 1969, and Supplement No. 9, Spring 1970. Reprinted with permission. Chapters 4 and 11 originally appeared in *Sisters Today* and are reprinted with permission. Chapter 5 originally appeared in *Catholic Mind* and is reprinted with permission. Chapter 10 is used with permission of the CICOP Meeting. Chapter 12 originally appeared in *Review for Religious*, Vol. 31 (1972) and is reprinted with permission. The lyrics for *Nowhere Man* are used with permission, copyright © 1965, Northern Songs Limited. All rights reserved.

Library of Congress
Catalog Card Number: 73-84049

ISBN 0-8091-1792-4

Published by Paulist Press
Editorial Office: 1865 Broadway, N.Y., N.Y. 10023
Business Office: 400 Sette Drive, Paramus, N.J. 07652

Printed and bound in the
United States of America

CONTENTS

FOREWORD

In times of major cultural change, Christian man becomes a pilgrim again, and his life in Christ becomes, more than ordinarily, a journey in the desert. One perspective on the Church after Vatican II is to see her, like Abraham, going forth at the call of God without quite knowing where she is going (Hebrews 11:8).

How are we to disengage Christian faith from the time-bound cultural expressions and vehicles of the past without loss of integrity? That is indeed the question at the heart of the anguish, tensions and polarizations characteristic of a period which has turned out to be as much a new Passion as a new Pentecost. No group in the Church has had to deal with the question with greater seriousness than members of religious communities, and particularly of American communities of religious women. In my opinion, these last represent the cutting edge of renewal and have yielded in the past several years the most courageous and intelligent leadership which we have in the Church today.

Most or all of the essays on religious life in this book speak with greater or lesser immediacy to the above question, particularly as recent cultural changes touch the basic ideas of secularization and personalism. It may be well briefly to indicate a few threads of unity among these several reflections.

The principal target of the first essay is a mentality, characterized as "essentialism," which lingers after the demise of the culture in which it thrived. As an approach to change in the religious life, it can lead, I think, only to sterility. Yet, as I try to show, we are not condemned to sheer situationism in renewing and adapting our life. Historical identity and contemporary discernment are the terms chosen to describe a mentality and method attentive to the unique history and mystery of persons and communities.

This essay makes it abundantly clear that the reader cannot expect in the following ones any clear definition of the religious life, but at most some enlightening pointers to its identity as a life-situation in the Church. The four following essays are partial efforts at such identification. The first of these takes off from Goffman's description of "total institution," so abhorrent to our contemporary insistence on personhood, goes on to show that "total community" is quite a different kind of relationship, and then affirms, in nonsacralistic terms, that a total sharing in depth of human existence, mediating our union with God, is characteristic of religious community. A similar effort to meet contemporary difficulties against religious life is made in the next essay, which sees religious life as verifying, paradoxically, whatever is valid in Bonhoeffer's call to "religionless Christianity." The two following essays also have secular Christianity for their context. "Consecration for Life" seeks to disengage the lifetime commitment and fidelity of religious from an outmoded canonization of permanency, by insisting that it is the *quality* of our love which finds expression in a vowed existence. "Responding to Secularization" reflects on the variety of ways in which religious may respond to the ambivalence of today's secular culture. Let the reader remember that it was written a long, long time ago (1968); he may find in the concluding essay of the book (previously unpublished) something of a *Retractatio*.

Pluralism of a twofold kind is the concern of the essay on styles of religious life. Even in 1973, the polarization of "charismatic" and "secular" types remains a major issue, and I, for one, have found no solution apart from a patient effort to understand those who dare to be different from ourselves. The "avant-garde or civil servant" discussion is less tense in its import; in fact, I personally find delight in this particular ambivalence or paradox.

The context of secularization is somewhat present in the essay on poverty, where an accent on personal presence to the poor represents a more sacral approach, while an accent on pragmatic service and influence is more illustrative of the secular component of Christian faith. The first essay on celibacy is, in effect, an effort to delineate the antisacralistic character of Christian celibacy, and of the Christian faith which it manifests. "A Love to Be Lived" reflects more of the personalistic mentality, though it might be said to be desacralizing in its insistence on the element of human passion in celibate love. Religious obedience finds no formal treatment of any length in this volume (though I would refer the reader to the brief treatment in the essay "Religious Community"). But the basic message of the essay, "Freedom Through Dependence," is easily applicable to religious obedience, and so is included here.

In reflecting on most of the essays here presented, I now see that the anthropological or humanistic approach is most prominent. This is legitimate enough, I feel, but I am glad that I can include two essays which touch on the reality for which the structures and style of religious life are mere mediations: man's finding God in the freedom of presence and the freedom of decision. My one regret is that there is no reflection in this volume on that which has ever been the heart of the life of the counsels: the following of Jesus Christ, an intense personal love for him who is both center and horizon of all we are and all we aspire to be as Christians and religious.

"Prospectus: Religious Life as Countercultural" says in rather general terms just where I personally am at the moment, at least in aspiration, and where I feel we are all called to be.

It may serve as a partial corrective for any too naive endorse-ment of secular Christianity which some of the previous essays may be guilty of. In calling for a more critical and apocalyptic stance toward the world around us, it may be saying that the most appropriate symbol for religious in the Church, as well as for Christians in society, is not the question mark, as an older eschatologism was inclined to say, nor the exclamation point, as tended to emerge from Teilhardian and personalistic enthusiasm, but that new and marvellous sign which best, I think, describes the mystery and excitement of this life: the *interrobang*.

For whatever is good in these pages, it is a joy to express my gratitude to my own "total community," the members of the Society of Jesus, especially those with whom I have lived, and also to the many religious men and women who have both inspired and received my efforts to put into words what they so courageously strive to put into the deeds and sufferings of a vowed life in Christ. I would like in a special way to thank two friends who encouraged the publication of some of my talks and articles on the religious life: the first is Fr. Catalino Arévalo, S.J., of Loyola House of Studies in the Philippines; the second is Robert Heyer of the Paulist Press, to whom I am also indebted for many editorial suggestions.

1

TWO MENTALITIES ON RENEWAL

It is impossible to define *religious life and unwise to look for its "essence." But it can be sufficiently* identified, *on the basis of its history and the contemporary call of the Spirit.*

For several years now a situation of tension has existed between the Sacred Congregation for Religious and some of the more creative groups among American sisters. This situation is important not just because of its possibly fateful implications for the future of religious life in America and elsewhere, but also because it involves two sharply contrasting mentalities on how change is to take place in the Church.

Several years ago, the Immaculate Heart Sisters of Los Angeles, a relatively small congregation, after lengthy and much publicized negotiations, eventually received a "shape up or ship out" ultimatum from the Congregation. The majority chose to "ship," so far as remaining "canonical religious" was concerned.

In 1970, American communities of contemplative women were presented with a similar harsh alternative. They were either to conform to a code (antiquated, in my opinion) of "enclosure," or else seek dispensation from their vows and start up afresh as a "pious union," without any ties with the community within which they had consecrated themselves for life. In 1971 a more particular action along similar lines was activated against contemplative Carmelite nuns.

The School Sisters of St. Francis, with headquarters in Milwaukee, also came under pressure from Congregation. In this case, too, the Roman authorities appeared to be following a "ship or shape" philosophy. The Franciscan Sisters were directed to show that their new life style could be reconciled with the religious life, and that it is supported by the documents of Vatican II. Otherwise, said the directive unblinkingly, "we would raise no objections to their following their convictions, but not inside the religious state."

Some were inclined to view these cases in terms of the personalities involved. They sighed for the retirement of the aging and ailing head of the Congregation, Cardinal Ildebrando Antoniutti. Or they were critical of the late Fr. Edward Heston, secretary of the Congregation, or of Fr. Bernard Ransing, a member, both of whom appeared periodically from Rome with official or quasi-official views to communicate.

Others see the problem as stemming, at least in part, from a certain ambiguity regarding the status of religious in the Church. The ambiguity has to do with the "public" character of religious profession. Religious have, on the one hand, traditionally brought their charismatic vocation to the official Church for its blessing. This is not a purely symbolic gesture, for there is a good deal of wisdom and discretion available, even and especially for pioneering groups, in the experience of the institutional Church. The fact that such guidance often appears prosaic and mediocre is a hard but inevitable fact in a sinful Church.

The other side of the coin, however, is that this blessing and guidance (not dissimilar from the service performed by the institutional Church with respect to the sacrament conferred on each other by the partners in marriage) can degenerate, especially where there is question of religious women, into a paternalistic and bureaucratic control that is incompatible with the distinctively free character of the call to follow the evangelical counsels. Religious can come to be viewed as situated halfway between clergy and laity, a view explicitly excluded by Vatican II's Constitution on the Church: "The religious state of life is not an intermediate one between the clerical and lay states" (n. 43); "The religious state . . . does not belong to the hierarchical structure of the Church" (n. 44).

Functionally, the misconception excluded by Vatican II can lead to the assumption that the fact of religious profession makes a sister an employee of the institutional Church. The freedom of a community to choose its fields of apostolic action easily becomes compromised, and it is but one step further for Church authorities to exercise a degree of control of the community in its inner aspect which, at least today, is unduly restrictive. We are now witnessing in the United States a strong reaction against such excessive control. The call sometimes heard for a massive opting out from canonical status is but one shrill expression of a growing impatience and despair.

The problem is compounded, as regards apostolate, when it is assumed that every apostolate chosen by a religious community or its individual members is automatically auxiliary to the apostolate of the bishops and priests. In this regard the distinction made by Vatican II's Constitution on the Church (n. 33) between the call of every baptized Christian to apostolate and the call of some to a more direct assistance to the bishops in their apostolate should be extended to religious, at least to those who are not clerics. Just as the secular layman needs no special permission to inaugurate, say, a clinic for psychological counseling, so there would seem to be no general need of special hierarchical direction and control of many of the works of religious.

It will, undoubtedly, take time for religious themselves as well as others to grow in understanding of these distinctions.

In the meantime, their blurring adds to the prevailing tensions.

These factors undoubtedly have a good deal to do with the present difficulties. It must be admitted, too, that religious communities are themselves seriously divided about the process of renewal, and that interventions from Rome are usually stimulated by communications from American sisters who view with alarm some of the more progressive trends taking place within their own communities. Nor should one fall into the trap of thinking that all wisdom is embodied in the proponents of radical change, or that only conservatives can be narrow and rigid.

Without denying the importance of all these considerations, I am convinced that there are, in the background, some largely unnoticed factors that transcend personalities and any misunderstanding of the role of religious in the Church. We are, in fact, in the presence of two basically different understandings of the renewal of the Church. What is fascinating from a theological point of view is to compare the workings of these divergent mentalities in the pastoral and doctrinal areas of the Church's life.

The Congregation for Religious, in-effect, sees religious life as an essence, primarily canonical in character. Enclosure, for example, is of the essence of contemplative life. And a fixed religious garb, while not of the essence of the religious life as such, belongs to the nature and characteristics of those communities that have adopted a habit. Religious communities in the proper sense have "left the world," whereas secular institutes are "in the world." There is, in other words, a certain set of specifics, a kind of checklist, which must guide the development of communities in this period of change.

Of course (and here is where the "ship or shape" tactics of the Congregation could be disastrous for religious life in our country), if a community or some individuals in it feel that they cannot conform to the duly designated specifics, there remains the possibility of a transformation into another essence. One does not have to be a "contemplative" or a "canonical religious." There are, after all, other categories, e.g., secular institutes, pious unions. Let the innovators get dispensed from their vows as contemplatives or as religious and start up again, following the specifics of another canonical essence. Only in this way—so runs the implicit reasoning of the Congregation's recent moves—may we preserve clear and distinct ideas regarding the specifically different vocations to the life of the counsels.

Now this essentialist and predominantly juridical mentality and methodology bear a striking resemblance to one theological view of how the Church's dogma develops. Once a dogma has been defined, according to this opinion, any subsequent efforts to deepen our understanding of the pertinent aspect of the Christian mystery must be checked out, in linear fashion, against the essential elements of the dogma. Conflicting conceptions and even clashing terminologies are discountenanced. Dogma is affirmed by the proponents of this position to be immutable. There lies at hand, they hold, a convenient tool for judging whether a contemporary theological exploration regarding, say, original sin or the Eucharist, is or is not within the bounds of orthodoxy. Clear dogmatic definition, especially when reaffirmed by the magisterium, is that tool.

The underlying concern of this mentality, both in pastoral and doctrinal matters, is a legitimate and even necessary one. Christian faith in its various aspects and embodiments must be, in any given era, identifiable. Radical and total discontinuity with the past would lead to a dissolution of Christian faith. This is true not only of doctrinal development, but also—with important differences—of the evolution of the various charismatic traditions that find expression in religious community.

But the essentialist response to this real problem is, in my opinion, too neat to be true or useful. Although Christian faith is and must be identifiable, it is—because it is mystery—not adequately definable. Its particular pastoral, as well as doctrinal, expressions do not admit of continuity by way of clear and distinct ideas. To deal with the mystery of Christ in any of its aspects as if it were an essence is to profane it. Unwittingly, the methodology followed by the Congregation for Religious, in the cases we have cited, runs the risk of just such a profanation.

But do we have an alternative methodology? We do, I believe. It is less tidy. It demands much more trust in persons and communities and above all in the Holy Spirit. But it does offer a viable alternative to the rigid approach outlined above and also to an amorphous drift into an unidentifiable future with which Rome is, quite understandably, much concerned.

I would characterize this alternative approach to renewal by the phrase, "historical identity and contemporary discernment." The approach has been admirably set forth, as regards doctrinal development, by Avery Dulles, S.J., in his important essay, "Dogma as an Ecumenical Problem," (*The Survival of Dogma*, New York, 1971). I see Fr. Dulles' reflections as pointing the way to a satisfactory method of dealing, not only with the thorny problem of doctrinal continuity, but also with the equally difficult questions of renewal and adaptation in the pastoral life of the Church. I wish to develop this approach here in the context of the recent tensions between American sisters and the Roman authorities.

Religious communities are best considered not as verifications of a species but as unique, historically identifiable communities of the evangelical counsels. Each has a founder or foundress, an initial vision of God's call to it, and some—always inadequate—expression of that vision in a basic rule and other primary documents, as well as in many nonconceptual symbols. Each community has a very particular history. In it the Spirit, constantly overcoming human sinfulness, has shaped the community toward his purpose. Each community arrives at the present juncture bearing its own history, a history that is normally both gift and burden.

What makes *this* community distinctive in comparison with other communities cannot be adequately grasped in objective terms. And while it may be convenient to group communities with similar characteristics according to several predominant types, one must always be wary of the "genus and species" syndrome. There is a concrete, existential identity that escapes neat definition. Yet it does not totally escape appropriate expression, conceptual and nonconceptual. A person knows who he is. A real community does, too, even though the effort to put it into words will always fall short of the mark.

Each religious community, while it is historically identifiable, is called to a contemporary discernment of what its future is to be. As it rereads its origins and its history, it also discerns the signs of our times. It also consults the Spirit to see just how it, with *its* (and no other) historical identity and contemporary situation, is to shape *its* expressions of the original vision, and also enrich that vision, as a genuine fidelity demands. Shall *this* community now, for the first time, branch out from formal education to engage in social work? Shall *this* community of religious brothers, for the first time, ordain a number of priests? Shall *this* community of contemplatives, for the first time, admit into its weekly program some visiting of the aged in a nearby home, or encourage its members to a writing apostolate?

As these questions are asked, who knows the answers except the Spirit? The answers cannot be had by sheer deduction from canonical premises. It is appropriate, of course, that sound experience and careful reflection should find, in due time, canonical expression, especially for the protection of the rights of persons and communities. But in a period of profound cultural and ecclesiastical change, when the law of the Church is itself in process of radical revision, a methodology that stolidly imposes canonical categories appropriate to a previous age on the movement of life is counterproductive, to say the least.

The present legal categories (institutes of religious, in the narrow sense, societies of common life, secular institutes, pious unions) are very questionably useful today for expressing the various charisms of celibate Christian communities. Normative appeal to them by Church authorities in order to handle problems of life and growth is at best an evasion and at worst a positive hindrance to the workings of the Spirit, who hasn't yet told us all that he has in mind for the future of religious life.

Does this proposed solution spell anarchy? Is any community free to make any change it wishes, to become whatever it wants to be? The methodology of historical identity and contemporary discernment does not lead to such amorphous results. Consulting the Spirit does not mean that one neglects history, rationality, pragmatic good sense. Communities, like persons, are always situated in their freedom. There are antecedent probabilities to be respected. There are inherent historical limitations which would make it folly for Community X to develop in one direction, or Community Y in another. Communities, like persons, are called to be faithful to their own past, a past that they bring with them into the future.

Will some communities discern badly and destroy themselves? Possibly some will. But all of them should be given the chance to discern wisely. And, especially in the case of religious women, the men of the Church must seriously ask themselves whether a lingering male chauvinism and protectionism is not still at work in this area. Why is it that it is communities of religious women, and not of religious men, who are the object of such nagging scrutiny on the part of the Congregation? Is there not an unconscious sex differential at work here?

All of this may make the present situation appear grim and hopeless. If this is not in fact the case, it is especially because among the major superiors of American religious women today there are to be found some of our most mature Christian leaders. One sign of this maturity is that they have not, like some others, called for the abolition of the Congregation for Religious, or for a massive opting out from canonical status on the part of American sisters. But neither are they passively acquiescing in the Congregation's sometimes unfortunate moves, as if these were automatically a sign of God's call. If the Congregation can be brought to see (and one can hope some American bishops will lend a hand) that a new methodology—one that is more respectful of personal freedom, subsidiarity and the element of mystery in religious community —is now called for, it can fulfill its role of service to religious and to the entire Church with greater, not less, influence.

2

RELIGIOUS COMMUNITY

As a free commitment to share human life in depth and quality with a particular group of persons, religious life may be described in terms of "total community."

Erving Goffman, a social scientist, has written an intriguing book entitled *Asylums: Essays on the Social Situation of Mental Patients and Other Inmates*. It is a study of what the author calls the "total institution," that is, "a place of residence and work where a large number of like-situated individuals, cut off from the wider society for an appreciable period of time, together lead an enclosed, formally administered round of life." One of the interesting things about the book is that among the "total institutions" studied, along with prisons, mental hospitals, military barracks, and the like, are abbeys, monasteries, convents and other cloistered residences. The portrait of religious community that results from such association is hardly flattering. The fact that the author draws predominantly on Kathryn Hulme's *The Nun's Story* for his image of religious community hardly helps the case. Still, Goffman's work is valuable as a stimulus to reflection on the nature and role of religious community considered precisely as community. When properly conceived and lived, this form of Christian life is far from being the drab, impersonal and totally demanding institution described in the pages of

Asylums. But if the term "total institution" is inappropriate for the life of the counsels in community, the term "total community" is, on the contrary, most apt. It is under this aspect of a total sharing of existence that the following paragraphs will explore the meaning of the religious life as community.

The meaning of "total community"

The term "community" is used for a great variety of human groupings. We speak of a community of scholars, a neighborhood community, the community of nations, and so forth. If community (*koinonia*) is taken as one of those primordial and almost mystical notions expressing what is most mysterious in human life, then it is clear that not all human groupings are equally deserving of the term. The more perfectly an association of humans verifies the idea of community, the less definable it becomes, and the less its character can be caught and expressed by speaking of its pragmatic function. The "community" of scientists, technologists, administrators and workers at Cape Kennedy, for example, can be defined, more or less, in terms of specific goals. An element of *esprit de corps* undoubtedly enters into the complexus of relationships; but basically the relationships are such as not to involve the person as person in the same way, for example, as in a close-knit family.

This transcendence of the merely functional or pragmatic in the higher types of human community must be appreciated if we are to grasp the sense in which a religious community is a total community. It is interesting and sometimes amusing to see a religious community struggling to express its identity in purely functional and objective terms. "What is it that distinguishes us from Congregation X or Y?" Precisely because religious community engages persons as persons with a certain totality, no objective formula will capture the identity of any particular community. The singularity of history, the distinctiveness of a charismatic founder and of a charismatic tradition, and a quality of depth and totality in the relationships which constitute the community, can be no more than hinted at in a verbal formulation.

This may also be the place to comment on another commonly discussed question. In recent years religious have been asking themselves, "Did we come together to *be* together, or to *do* something together?" Either horn of the dilemma has its shortcomings. If one opts for *being*, he (or the community) is open to the charge of navel-gazing while the people perish of hunger. And it is quite correctly pointed out that most founders and foundresses were seized by a palpable need in their milieu, an evil to be remedied, a good to be achieved, and not by any fondness for being or for being-community. If one chooses, however, a functional understanding of religious community, there are the opposite pitfalls. No community can identify itself as community merely by the kind of work it does. And the temptation exists to conceive and speak of community as a means to an end. This deplorable phrase tends to overlay the fact that a community is not a thing, nor is it merely the sum total of the persons who are its members. Community is a reality of the order of personhood, a value in itself, never to be made a mere tool for the achievement of anything outside itself, however worthwhile the goal may be.

Probably the option between *being* and *doing* is a bad way of conceiving community. The danger of applying such generic categories to persons and to communities of persons is that one may fail to respect the element of mystery and transcendence. This is not to deny that, in the explicit motivation or in the enduring style of religious communities, there can be, and are, notable differences from the viewpoint of prayer and action, inner community life and apostolate. One might perhaps see here one of the ways of distinguishing different major types of communities. Surely there is a difference of accent or blend between the communities of the great monastic and contemplative traditions and the post-tridentine congregations of nurses and teachers. It remains, however, that both *being* and *doing* will be inseparably joined in all forms of genuine community, just as they are within the individual human person. For community is nothing but persons related as persons, that is, in knowledge and love. Community shares in the quality of mystery which belongs to the person.

Religious community: a family?

The comparison of the religious community with the community of marriage and family raises difficulties for many today. Some would consider that a community of friends, or a scientific or technological team, or a business corporation, offers a more appropriate model. In the traditional image (especially monastic, perhaps) of the religious community as a family or brotherhood living in obedience to one father-figure, who stands both for God and for the community, they see the subtle danger of prolonging the *infantilisme* so much deplored in recent writings on the religious life. Unlike the family, the religious community is made up exclusively of adults. Unlike the family, entry into the community, on the part of all members, is the result of free choice.

There are, certainly, limitations in this model of religious community. But marriage, especially in the horizontal dimension, that is, in the relationship of husband and wife, possesses what the other suggested models (with the exception of the model of friendship) do not: a depth of mystery which finds expression in the related qualities of totality and irrevocability. In this it remains the best analogue of religious community.

Whatever the pressures to which it is subject today, marriage in the Christian view, both as a human reality and as participating in the mysterious marriage of Christ and his Church, represents a total and irrevocable sharing of life by two human persons. The term "contract" is less appropriate than the term "covenant": and precisely for this reason, that contract suggests a delimited area of function within which the partners oblige themselves to certain modes of action; whereas the term covenant, particularly in its rich biblical connotations, conveys a bestowal of *self* that is in principle without limit. To conceive of the relationship of marriage as an accumulation of rights and duties touching marital intercourse, other signs of affection, cohabitation, financial assistance, and so forth, is to miss the woods for the trees. What gives life to each of these specific responsibilities of married people is that they are the expression and vehicle of a more basic and total relationship. Some years ago, the film *Marty* portrayed with both humor and poignancy the anguish of the typical bachelor drawn toward marriage, yet reluctant to leave behind his pleasant relationships with "the boys." Perhaps Marty's basic fear was not so much that he would no longer be able to play billiards or have a few congenial beers in a male environment, but that he would be involved in sharing the *whole* of his life with someone else.

The conditions of total community

Just what is meant in this context by the phrase "total community"? It conveys range, depth, and quality. Unlike the relationship of the team or work group, total community means that the relationship with the other radiates into the whole of life, with no area excepted. It is a commitment through which the totality of existence is shared. If a man were to conceive, for example, that his choices of a job and friends are matters outside the marriage covenant, he would not be accepting marriage as a total community. This is not to say that he will necessarily talk over with his wife the decision to change his employment. As we will see when we come to speak of the religious community as such, the specific expressions of a relationship of total community and the relationship itself are not simply identical, even though there must be mutual interaction between the two. The point here is that total community is unlimited in scope; the whole range of human endeavor lies within commitment to it.

Depth is another characteristic of total community. The decision to enter it and the daily ratifications of it differ from other options, even from very important ones, in that they have a certain irrevocability. "I, John, take you, Mary, for better or worse . . . until death." The only limits to this kind of engagement are those over which we have no control. So far as the persons making the engagement are concerned, they have placed firmly behind them the possibility of ever being apart, once this consent to be together has been uttered. We know that the Spirit, in the mystery of his providential wisdom, does sometimes introduce separation, usually painful and often tragic. Death, and certain incapacitating physical or psychological diseases, such as insanity or alcoholism, are some of the familiar modes of parting. But these do not form qualifying conditions placed on the consent itself, and do not reduce the irrevocable character of the consent.

Finally, the *quality* of relationship in total community distinguishes it from all other forms of community, in that the person as person is fully engaged, and the relationship itself is characterized by the unconditioned presence to one another of the partners in the covenant. There are others which demand a measure of mutual fidelity; but because these affect the contracting parties less deeply, the persons involved are less immanent in their mutual pledges. With total community, however, each person brings himself in a qualitatively higher way to the relationship, which is itself completely different from the partial sharings of other relationships. As nothing (no *thing*) can be compared with a person, so no diminished form of sharing personal life can be compared with total community.

Personal conscience and total community

Before moving on to speak of religious community as a verification of total community, two difficulties must be dealt with. The first would question the very morality of total community as described here, on the grounds that one may never morally escape the demands of conscience. Personal conscience, it is alleged, will sometimes lead an individual to disagree with his community. This is perfectly true; but it would be a mistake to conceive that such cases call for a restriction in the basic covenant itself. Far from a conscientious dissent, however painful, being a reservation placed on total commitment, it is an implicit exigency of that commitment, and actually enhances it. I owe it to my beloved community to disagree with it when I see clearly, in the Spirit, that it is not, in a particular action or even in an habitual mode of its existence, walking according to the Spirit. It should also be recalled that the community too, as a corporate person, has its conscience. And just as its commitment to me is not limited but rather enlarged by its corrective function toward me, so my acceptance of life in it as a total community is without limit.

Is total community possible?

The second difficulty against the concept of total community is that it demands too much from frail human beings.

Since we are not angels, tentativeness is characteristic of all we do, and the deepest human fidelity would seem to be tinged necessarily with at least a faint hue of "unless." There is a real truth in the difficulty. Except in death, no human promise is absolutely irrevocable in fact. We can always go back on our word. In addition, fidelity as a virtue or attitude is less a possession to be retained than a treasure for which we strive. We *become* faithful much more than we *keep* fidelity. Nevertheless, there is a real difference between a mere declaration of intention, however serious, and the pledge or promise whose quality is that of covenant and not of mere contract. Though the resulting relationship is shot through with our human frailty, this quality coexists with a certain firmness and irrevocability. It is the simultaneity of this weakness and strength which gives to total community, as a community of covenant, a singular beauty which men have always recognized and always will.

The counsels and total community

We have already drawn several implications about religious community as total community. But much more remains to be said. First, we must point out that not every community of prayer and apostolic action in the Church needs to be, or is in fact, total community in the sense described above. This is an important point to realize today, when there are signs that a good number of Christians, some of them already religious, are unwilling or unable to commit themselves to a particular total community of the counsels. There are other groupings in the Church within which they can both develop their Christian personhood and be of service to others. Once their incompatibility with the religious form of Christian life is clear, even if they have, unfortunately, already made profession of it, it will be a blessing for all concerned if they are allowed or persuaded to go another way. Nor should we be overly distressed if, in the coming decades, proportionately fewer Christians experience the call to total community within the religious life. It would be folly if, for the sake of keeping numbers up and staffing existing institutions, the element of total community were to be diluted or compromised.

Secondly, it is through a vowed embracing of the counsels that one enters upon this form of total community. By religious profession a baptized Christian pledges to God and man (immediately to the members of his community, more broadly to the entire Church) that he will share human life in its totality with the group of baptized Christians who are members of this community. And the community, in its turn, together with each of the other members, makes the same pledge. It is important to attend to this aspect of mutuality in the religious profession. In recent years, the profession ceremony of some communities has been giving it symbolic expression, with the religious superior, or all the members present, pledging themselves to receive the new member and support him in his effort to live his own commitment.

Just what express form the commitment to total community will take is an important but secondary matter. Traditionally, the triad of poverty, celibacy and obedience has been more common. The reality signified by these three must be present for this kind of total community, even when the formula of profession does not make explicit every member of the triad. It may be worth while here to specify how each of the three verify the notion of commitment to total community or a totally shared existence.

I would conceive, first of all, that by the commitment to a celibate life in community I agree to share my human affection with the members of the community. This implies not only that I commit myself to a special love for each member of the community and for the community as such, but that all other human loves in my life are to be measured against this prior commitment to love. My love for the community is not exclusive in the sense that I may love no one else, at least not intimately. It may in fact happen that my most intimate love will be directed to someone outside the community. My love for the community retains priority, however, in the sense that any such particular love, however noble in itself, must constantly be justified, in its beginning and in its enduring presence, with reference to the covenant of love I have made with the community. Here the contrast with the marriage covenant is illuminating. Both the marital and the celibate Christian community are characterized by a love that is both particular and universal. Married people are called to love each other and to love mankind. Members of the celibate Christian community are called to love one another and to love mankind. But the order of love is different. For the husband or wife, the prior commitment, against which further possible commitments must be measured, is the particular one, not the universal one. For the religious, the opposite is the case: his word of love has been addressed to the community he enters (which stands for him as the Church and mankind generally). When particular loves offer themselves, they will be received or not according as they conflict with or deepen his covenant with his community.

Total community verifies itself in the vow of poverty as a covenant to share one's material goods, work, talents, and also the corresponding privations, with the members of this community. The particular traditional prescriptions regarding permissions, common life (in the sense of seeking the fulfillment of one's material needs from the community, not from elsewhere), a frugal existence, etc., are simply forms in which the basic will to share human existence finds expression and support in this specific area of human life. Obviously there is a wide range of such particular forms possible and desirable, provided the net result is a totally shared existence.

Obedience is the counsel and vow in which, perhaps, the

element of totality in religious community is most prominent and also most challenging. For obedience touches precisely the area of freedom and decision, and what total community is all about is a freely chosen sharing of life in all its dimensions. My profession of obedience is, obviously, not an abdication of my freedom of conscience. It is, however, the expression of a willingness to share the decisions of my life with my community. No area or kind of decision is excepted from this radical commitment to share life with others. How I care for my health, how much I travel, the clothes I wear, how much I pray, what I do with my money, what dealings I have with my friends outside the community: all these decisions I have agreed to share with my fellow religious.

Some objections

I am sure that this understanding of the vows, especially the vow of obedience, as an irrevocable and total commitment to share affection, goods and decisions with a particular group of human beings, will make some people nervous. They will recall, perhaps, the stunting and even the destruction of personhood which they have witnessed in religious communities, and they will wonder whether the term, "total community," is not just a novel substitute for "surrender of one's own will and judgment," "holocaust of obedience," "death to self," in the name of which human beings have been irreparably damaged in their chance for personal growth. How, the objection may be phrased, can total community fail to lead to total institution, in Goffman's sense?

The difficulty is a real one, and would merit a fuller and deeper treatment than can be given here. Two responses, the second less superficial than the first, will be offered. First, it is imperative, as we indicated when speaking of total community in general, that we distinguish between the basic covenant or covenant relationship and the particular forms in which it is manifested and sustained. The character of totality, irrevocability, absoluteness, about which we are talking, inheres in the basic relationship, not in the forms. For example, the fact that I have committed myself to share my use of material goods with others does not imply that I have the same diet as my fellow religious, or get my wardrobe from some common tailor. It does not exclude, for example, that there be an understanding that a religious working for a salary in some secular institution would have a bank account, pay certain bills himself, and in general proceed with only rare instances in his life of having to ask special permissions regarding the use of funds. The same distinction between the radical relationship and, on the other hand, the concrete actualizations of the relationship of mutual dependence and sharing between individual and community holds for celibacy and obedience. Cultural and psychological factors will affect just what expressions of radical and total sharing are appropriate. That there will be *some* expression goes without saying, since basic relationships cannot be maintained without appropriate expression. A man who never kissed his wife would, normally, hardly be maintaining his basic covenant with her; but this does not determine anything at all regarding the frequency and regularity of this gesture of love. So with the gestures which express and thereby confirm the love relationship of a religious community. Today, quite necessarily, we are in process of reducing the number and regularity of our common gestures of solidarity. Undoubtedly some individuals and communities will go too far in this reaction to the excessive controls operative in the past, and we will probably have to rediscover that some degree of regular rhythm and of stability is indispensable if any human community is to be lasting. But we have had too much evidence of the tragedies that can result when forms of living are absolutized. Ideally, at least, freedom to change the forms, far from putting pressure on the totality of our basic commitment, is necessary if that commitment is not to become a tedious burden and an irrelevancy.

A more basic response to the objection against total community as running the risk of total institution is simply to acknowledge the presence of this risk, and to say that without it the specific contribution of the life of the counsels in community cannot be realized. What is impossible to man is possible to God. With the incarnation, death and resurrection of Jesus Christ something absolutely new has come into the world. Apart from him, and precisely as sinners, we do well to guard our individual freedom against the threat of the crowd. This is precisely what original sin is in the social dimension: it is irreconcilable mutual hostility in which the group threatens my freedom, and vice-versa. It is alienation of the most desperate kind, in which it is impossible to trust one another. While we are sinners, there is simply not the possibility of a total community that would not be in reality a total institution, a destruction of persons (and therefore of community) in the faceless crowd.

It is the hallmark of the paschal mystery that alienation is healed through the very instruments of alienation. Evil is not so much simply removed as reversed in its direction. The condition of a man's finding the reconciled and reconciling community (apart from which he cannot find the reconciling God in Christ), is that he accept the risk of experiencing the crowd, and in fact experience it. It is such a risk that is inherent in being a Christian in the first place, and the risk is intensified when one becomes a religious. I have no guarantee that my community will not act toward me as a crowd, nor for that matter, can the community guarantee that I will not be an anarchist toward it. Humanly speaking, this total community which is the religious life is an unlikely proposition. It can work only in the extraordinary happening of the will to continual conversion, the will to reconciliation, desired and lived by individuals and by the community as a whole. And because this total community is not natural in the sense in which the total community of marriage and family is natural, its success should always come as something of a surprise. People today tend to get discouraged at its seeming to work so rarely and so imperfectly. If we realized how many human obstacles there are to its working well, we might be more grateful for the enormous contribution it has made to Christian and to human life. And we religious might be more grateful for the fact that we are the ones called and empowered to live it. If human beings are made for communion in depth and constancy, then this life of total celibate community, though not the only way or the best way for all, remains a thrilling (because improbable) and secure (because dependent on the power of God) way to realize such communion.

3

THE LIFE OF THE COUNSELS: RELIGIONLESS CHRISTIANITY

In the tradition of Luther, who criticized religious vows as inimical to "justification by faith," Bonhoeffer's call for "religionless Christianity" might seem to threaten the life of the counsels. But could it be that this life is, on the contrary, a special witness to justification by faith and a kind of "religionless Christianity"?

Few Roman Catholics have doubted, till recently at least, the appropriateness of the term, "religious," as it is applied to those who consecrate themselves to God in lifelong poverty, chastity and obedience. If religion is man's relation to God, who in the world—by inner consecration and visible worship to God's word and offer of life—would seem to verify the notion of "religious" better than those men and women in the Church whose very existence is specified by its concern for the things of the Lord?

Yet there is a genuine sense in which "religious" are called to challenge and even destroy "religion," not to exemplify it. In the context of a Church in the throes of renewal and reform, and of a world disillusioned with the products of religion, a plausible case can be made for discreetly dropping this traditional term in speaking of the charism of celibate Christian community.

This proposal will seem less startling if one reflects, first of all, on how Jesus and his first disciples stood toward the contemporary religious establishment, Jewish and pagan. The Synoptics and John disclose that the deadly enemies of Jesus were not libertines or agnostics but the most respected religious leaders of his time. We find that the constant direction of his preaching and practice is to relativize the existing religious code, cult and creed. He designates a purer faith, by which men would serve God in spirit and truth and with compassion for the needy, rather than by a devout presence in the temple, as the touchstone of man's acceptance by God. It would be a distortion, to be sure, to depict Jesus, as some have done, as a reformer of secular life or to neglect the primacy in his life and preaching of absolute obedience to the will of an all-loving Father. It remains, however, that he stood among his contemporaries as anything but a "religious" figure, and that the accusation which led to his execution was precisely blasphemy, *the* sin against religion.

A very similar picture emerges when one studies the writings of the apostle Paul, especially in such polemical works as *Galatians*. Paul did have occasion to rebuke those early Christians who took advantage of the freedom Christ had won for them to live irreligiously, in the conventional sense. But he was much more concerned to keep the impressionable young churches he had founded free from the pseudo-religious attitudes and practices of the judaizers, that is, those early converts from Judaism who would not or could not quite believe that the messianic promises now reposed in a universal family drawn from Jew and Gentile alike, regardless of racial descent or ritual practice. We shall return later in this essay to examine more in detail the Pauline attack on this effort to convert the good news of justification by faith into a self-glorifying religion radically opposed to that good news.

Historical scholarship has, for a long time, been aware that the early Christians were viewed with suspicion by religious contemporaries. There was a genuine basis to the charge of many that Christians were "atheists." The God of Christians, the God of our Lord Jesus Christ, was no tribal god made to the tribe's image and having as his function the projection of the tribe's self-image into the sphere of ultimate meaning. He was a God without consort, a God for all men, a God whose involvement in human life through his son Jesus took place without compromise of his mysterious otherness. And he was a God who could be celebrated only by those who, in radical discipleship, were willing to walk the road to death and resurrection. As such he called men out of security to the pilgrim journey of faith. No wonder he did not meet the current qualifications for divinity. No wonder his people were considered enemies of religion.

It is against the background of such beginnings that one can best appreciate the language and the intent of recent theologians, particularly Karl Barth and Dietrich Bonhoeffer, when they speak pejoratively of "religion," and "being religious," and favorably of "religionless Christianity." A brief examination of what these two famous Protestant theologians are about will serve as useful context for our presentation of the life of the counsels.

Barth's attack on "religion" began, appropriately, in his celebrated commentary on *Romans*, and was continued, in somewhat more systematic form, in his *Church Dogmatics*.[1] What does Barth mean by "religion"? The answer is not so easy, for, contrary to the over-simplified version of his teaching often presented, he does not always view religion pejoratively. He does, however, begin his study of it by contrasting it with revelation. Whereas the term "revelation" is expressive of God's initiative and gracious self-communication to sinful man through his Word, "religion" is sinful man's effort to

[1] Karl Barth, *Church Dogmatics*, vol. 1, part 2, n. 17, "The Revelation of God as the Abolition of Religion," pp. 280-361.

reach out for God with an initiative that anticipates the divine action. At the risk of missing Barth's nuances and reading into his paragraphs connotations alien to his thought, we might equate religion in his usage with the Pelagian and semi-Pelagian stance, and also with the attitude of justification by works or merit (as opposed to justification by faith through grace) which Paul excoriates in *Romans* and *Galatians*. For Barth, then, the "religious" posture is man's search for God undertaken in disregard of God's prior finding of man in the sending of his Son and Spirit. Religion in this sense stands for contempt of the gift-character of the economy of salvation. For Barth, revelation does not link up with a human religion already present and practiced but rather contradicts it.

It is true, as we have indicated, that Barth does not always speak pejoratively of religion. His thesis conceives the Church as the locus of true religion. Still, she is this only in a dialectically qualified sense, similar to the sense in which we may legitimately speak of the justified sinner (*simul justus et peccator*). It is through grace that the Church lives by grace, and only to that extent is she the locus of true religion. Revelation is thus both judgmental and reconciling; it is man with his blasphemous "religion" that God reconciles and saves.

Bonhoeffer, who derives much from Barth, does not simply repeat the latter's critique of religion; in fact, Barth himself comes under the critique of the later Bonhoeffer. But in an earlier work, *The Cost of Discipleship*, Bonhoeffer has not yet come to his conception of "religionless christianity." Nor is it the threat of semi-Pelagianism which is his main concern. On the contrary, he severely criticizes the excesses or distortion of his own Lutheran tradition of "justification by faith." His impassioned contrast of "cheap grace" and "costly grace" sees in the former the unwillingness or inability to acknowledge that faith calls for works, that true discipleship includes obedience as well as faith. His accent, then, is just the opposite of what we have seen in Barth. It is in this connection that

Bonhoeffer pays tribute to but also criticizes monasticism. The monks, he says, were Christian in realizing that grace was costly, but they erred in making the road of costly grace the prerogative of an elite, instead of the vocation of all the baptized. One hears in this echoes of Luther's polemic.

Later, in his *Letters and Papers from Prison*, Bonhoeffer has changed his accent, and has to some extent transcended the dialectic of faith and works in his concern for a Christian faith responsive to the needs of contemporary man. Here, like Barth, he attacks "religion," but understands by it something different from Barth, and something more complex. Religion for Bonhoeffer means: (1) Individualism or the mystique of inwardness, an asceticism which, in the quest of private salvation, abandons the world to itself; (2) metaphysics, understood here not in the sense of the philosophy of being, but rather as the view that there is another world necessarily completing this one, that God or the divine is the superstructure for being, and that reality must somehow be completed by the "supernatural"; (3) a province of life, a religious *a priori*, a border existence, religion as a "sphere"; (4) a *deus ex machina*, God as the provider of answers for man's problems, with the result that actual godlessness is covered up with pietism and religiousness; (5) privilege, so that the *ek-klesia* becomes not those who are called out but the favored ones, an elite which enjoys the luxury of devotion. Such pseudo-religion is for Bonhoeffer just the opposite of Christ and the faith which he bestows on his disciples. Against individualism Christ is "the man for others"; against "metaphysics" he is lonely and forsaken without escape in the transcendent; against religion as a province of life he stands for worship in the midst of life; against the *deus ex machina* he does not experience the God of rescue.

What is common to both Barth and Bonhoeffer in their rejection of "religion" is a contrast between it and Christian faith. They both stand in the mainstream of the Reformation tradition, which makes the acceptance and proper understanding of justification by faith normative. And it is in terms of justification by faith that we must understand the life of the counsels. Our present concern is to show that the religious life, far from conflicting with the mentality of justification by faith, far from being "religious" in the sense in which Barth and Bonhoeffer blame it, represents in the Church a very special witness against "religion" and for justification by faith. It would be obviously absurd to understand this statement as attributing to religious a deeper faith than other Christians. What is in question here is a basic human and Christian situation, a life-form, a situational grace. The contention is that the life of the counsels lived in ecclesial community is, precisely as a life-form, a special verification of and witness to the Pauline doctrine of justification by faith.

What does Paul mean when he speaks of justification by faith, as he does especially in *Romans* and *Galatians*? In abbreviated form we may say that he is understanding faith as a total personal response to God revealing himself to sinful man, with special accent on the acknowledgment of man's inability to save himself without the gracious and free initiative of God in Christ Jesus. It is only in the acknowledgment of his own poverty and weakness, says Paul, that man can be enriched by God. And to accept salvation from God means to accept that man has nothing of his own in which he is able to boast over against God. "What do you have that was not given to you? And if it was given, how can you boast as though it were not?" (1 Cor 4, 7). For Paul, nothing is so inimical to the spirit of the Gospel as the spirit of the self-made man. And no attitude is more appropriate for the Christian disciple than gratitude, which recognizes that all is grace, all is gift.

Why do we maintain that the life of the counsels is a special verification of and witness to this central Pauline doctrine? Primarily because in following the life of the counsels, a Christian freely puts himself, at the divine call, in a basic human and Christian situation in which salvation (read "human fulfillment"), if it comes at all, will come clearly not from the merely immanent unfolding of human resources but from the power and wisdom of God. This will appear if one regards the commitment to celibacy, poverty and obedience from the viewpoint of the renunciation and risk involved. Ordinarily, it is through marriage and family, property (or its equivalent in contemporary society) and personal independence that man finds his way to human fulfillment. Written deep in the humanity of each one of us is the powerful drive to fulfill oneself in the intimacy of marital and parental love, and, especially in order to achieve this, to deal creatively with the material world and to develop one's personal autonomy. There is always an element of tragedy when this magnificent potential is frustrated for an individual (the eunuch, the psychological bachelor) or for large groups (the under-privileged classes, races and nations). Apart from the call of transcendence, we quite rightly are distressed or suspicious when a man or woman is unwilling or unable to embark on this adventurous road of human fulfillment. And all too often we witness with a sense of tragedy how lives can be stunted in the absence of a fulfilling family relationship.

To follow the call of the counsels, therefore, is not only renunciation but also risk. It is to put oneself in a situation which, apart from faith, offers only privation, not fulfillment. The very meaning of this situation is, then, to verify that human fulfillment (read "salvation") is the gift of God, and not an autonomous human achievement.

We are not in the least suggesting that only the celibate Christian community lives by faith, or even that it lives by a deeper faith. The religious profession is but a deepening of the baptismal profession, in which *every* Christian decides to risk human fulfillment for the sake of the Gospel. It is obviously true also that many married Christians live out of faith with a much greater intensity and depth than many religious.

It remains, however, that the two situations are not entirely parallel. Even prior to the call of the Gospel to live by faith, marriage is inscribed in our humanity; celibacy is not. Only if Christ is risen, only if his kingdom be the destiny of mankind, does this life-form as such make sense.

The life of celibate Christian community is, then, a special form of "religionless Christianity," in the sense that, as a life-situation, it verifies and witnesses to the fact that human fulfillment, justification, salvation, is the gift of God. In this sense, it is preeminently a life of *faith*. It is possible to explore this aspect of the life of the counsels by showing how each of the three counsels is a mediation of faith, and, as a basic attitude, almost identical with faith.

First, virginity or celibacy is an embodiment of faith. Within the New Testament itself there would seem to be no explicit connection made between faith and the praise of virginity. Yet those who make themselves eunuchs for the kingdom of heaven do so quite obviously from a motive of faith. (Cf. Mt 19, 12.) And Paul's praise of virginity couples it with concern for the Lord's affairs (1 Cor 7, 32; 7, 34).

In the Fathers of the Church, there is a close connection between the theme of virginity and that of faith. St. Augustine conceives that it is by faith (or by faith, hope and charity) that the entire Church and each of her members verify the notion of virginal motherhood. The special class of *virgines* is thus giving special witness to a faith-virginity which is characteristic of the whole Church. We may note also Augustine's stress on *humility* as a basic virtue characteristic of the true virgin. This humility is not just a modest opinion of oneself, but the acknowledgment that whatever grace one has is God's gift. Thus Augustinian humility and Pauline faith are akin.

The notion of *poverty* is also related intimately to the notion of faith and equally opposed to self-justifying "religion." This is true especially if we broaden the notion beyond con-

cern for the Christian use of material things, and conceive it
according to the biblical notion of the *anawim*. These are, it
will be recalled, those men and women who, in the midst of
social and economic privation, remain faithful to God and
put all their trust in his undying fidelity, not in human resources. The attitude of the *anawim* thus practically coin-
cides with that of Pauline faith, and is the opposite of self-
glorifying religiosity. From this viewpoint, too, "religious"
are called to be anything but "religious." Commitment to a
celibate existence in a celibate community, with the congruous
commitment regarding material goods (poverty in the nar-
rower sense) and regarding personal independence (obedience), puts a Christian in a special *anawim* situation: in the
experience of human privation he is to look to God alone for
fulfillment. Once again, the counsels are seen to verify Pauline
faith, not Barthian "religion."

Obedience is explicitly related to faith by Paul. (Cf. Rom
1, 5; 16, 26.) This use of the term obedience in connection
with faith highlights the fact that the directive principle of the
disciple's life is the invisible God through his Spirit, and not
autonomous self-direction. From this point of view, the instrument of expression of this radical faith-obedience to God
in the life of the counsels is the celibate *community*, a community of ignorant sinners, especially as represented through
the bearers of authority. When the celibate Christian entrusts
his destiny to the human weakness of such a community,
and does so at the special call of the Spirit, he is exercising
a faith-obedience which is the direct opposite of "religion."
Other human communities come together on the basis of
natural attractiveness and rich human resources. This community comes together, on the contrary, on the basis of human poverty and weakness, with the members hoping against
hope that God's power and wisdom will manifest itself.

The religious life is a life of the counsels under *vow*, or
some equivalent binding consecration. Very legitimately it

may be asked: Does the *vow* of lifetime celibacy, poverty and obedience not go contrary to the doctrine of justification by faith? One must confess that there is a way of speaking of the security of the religious life which invites religious themselves and others to view this life as a kind of insurance policy. But it need not be so. Furthermore, if one looks at the inherent dynamism of the life itself, in contrast to the motivation of any given individual (and what form of life cannot be distorted or corrupted by wrong motivation?), then it must be said that a vowed Christian existence is a special verification of and witness to justification by faith. The lifetime vow puts one in the condition of insecurity and risk, not of smug security. The commitment to fidelity until death in the way of the counsels is not a cautious contract with a party on whom one makes demands corresponding to one's own commitment, but, like the marriage vows, a covenant of fidelity "for better or for worse, for richer or for poorer, in sickness and in health, until death." The element of risk in faith is enhanced by the fact that the partner is the unseen Lord. There is reliance on his promise to bring fulfillment, but this confidence is at the opposite pole from the assurance arising from a contractual relationship. From every point of view, then, the religious life goes directly contrary to what Barth describes as "religion," that is, a quest for fulfillment in God undertaken from a purely human initiative and in reliance on human resources. It is no mere hankering to be contemporary which prompts the statement that the vowed life of the counsels is a distinctive form of "religionless Christianity," that is, of existence in Christian faith.

But what of Bonhoeffer's understanding of "religion" and of its opposite in true discipleship? I will leave it to the reader to reflect, in the light of what has already been said, on whether and how the life of the counsels is opposed to each of the five elements in Bonhoeffer's notion of "religion." I personally have no doubt of the results of such an analysis.

Someone has pointed out that there is a certain affinity between the genuine mystic and the atheist or agnostic: both insist on putting aside or leaving behind any divinity shaped to man's image, any god who is merely the projection of aspirations for which man is unwilling to take responsibility. Not every religious is a mystic, but the very structure of religious life, as a constant invitation to base one's fulfillment not on the seen, the heard, the felt, but on the power of the invisible God, draws one to plunge into that "dark night" which is the lived equivalent of the classic "negative theology"— the only genuine "Christian atheism."

This brings us, finally, to the important question whether the celibate Christian community has anything special to say to the world of today, particularly in the context of secularization, the secular mission of the Church, and the challenge posed by atheistic humanism, both as ideology and as lived human existence. The answer, as I see it, is a decided affirmative, on condition that religious communities really fulfill their role as a focus of radical Christian faith and as a battering ram against what Barth and Bonhoeffer describe as "religion." Within the Church, first of all, a dynamic life of the counsels can provide that sometimes disturbing, always challenging invitation to the entire Church really to be the pilgrim people of God, never settling down in comfortable security through fixed forms and formulations of the faith. From this point of view, religious life is intended as an antidote for piousity, for social quietism, for the elitism which always tempts some in the Church.

To those outside the Church, as well as to the important minority within the Church which is being tempted, in one way or another, to reduce the Church's contribution to human life to a bland semi-theism or to radicalism conceived in purely humanistic terms, the life of celibate Christian community also has something to say. It witnesses to the paschal mystery, to the need of walking the road of faith-poverty, faith-virginity and faith-obedience, if the human person and the community of mankind are to realize their potential. From this point of view, what the religious life contributes is a lived refutation of the charge, which one finds in various forms in Marx, Proudhon, Sartre and many others, that man abdicates his birthright when he plunges into the mystery of God. Faith is not religion; the journey in the night to find the God who is man's true future is no flight from the world; and the sacred pledge to live as celibate, poor and obedient Christians until death is a magnificent witness that justification comes by faith.

The witness is indeed magnificent, but we religious are anything but magnificent! How oppressed we are today with this sorry realization. The answer, however, is not in an orgy of self-recrimination, or in sad, sad prophecies of the demise of this form of the Christian life. What Karl Rahner has said of the issue of priestly celibacy is also true of the life of the counsels in religious community. Let us not ask about the survival of religious life in general. Let each one of us who is a religious ask *himself* about the depth and quality of his own commitment. *I* must ask *myself* whether I understand and live my commitment in religiosity or in faith. I must be honest enough to acknowledge that there has been too much religiosity and too little faith. And I must plead with the Lord, as one who desires, at least, to recognize his radical poverty: "Lord, I do believe. Please help me in my unbelief."

4

CONSECRATION FOR LIFE: THE CRISIS OF PERMANENCY

Not a cherishing of permanency as such, but the quality and depth of a love committed to God and man, is what finds expression and support in the lifetime vows of religious.

I understand the term "consecration for life" in a twofold sense: First, in the sense of a lifetime dedication, a covenant of fidelity with the Lord till the hour of death. And secondly, in the sense of a consecration whose very meaning is life, not death; enrichment, not diminishment. I understand this distinction in somewhat the same fashion as the scripture scholars understand the beautiful opening of chapter thirteen of Saint John's Gospel: "Having loved his own who were in the world, he loved them to the very end of his life." But this statement may also mean, "Having loved his own who were in the world, he loved them to the uttermost limits of his love, with deathless love." In the first sense, consecration for life is a question of how long, a question of duration, of quantity. In the second and more profound sense, consecration for life is a question of how deep, a question of intensity, of quality. Both questions are important, and both are difficult. I will be suggesting that to win any adequate answer to the first question we must explore the mystery of the second. And I will be suggesting that our real problem with commitment today is not permanency but quality and depth.

Let us begin by examining the first question—permanency. The last several years have raised for American religious men and women a whole series of questions touching the enduring character of the religious consecration, especially as this consecration finds expression in the three traditional vows of religion. It is important, I think, that we distinguish several questions now being asked, some of them far more fundamental than others.

First, there is the question whether consecration to the life of the counsels needs to find expression precisely in vows, that is, in promises of a sacred and juridically binding character made to God in the presence of the Church to follow the life of the counsels. Canonically, the present law of the Church (Canon 488) considers as religious in the strict sense only those who take vows. Religious institutes in this strict sense are thus distinct from societies of men and women living a common life without vows.

After the promulgation of the Code of 1918, the Church recognized secular institutes, so that another kind of evangelical life came into being without the necessity of vows. This canonical distinction, while insisted on in such documents as the *Instruction on the Renewal of Religious Formation* (1969), is widely regarded today as of secondary importance. In Vatican II, the decree *Perfectae Caritatis,* even though it mentions the distinction (n. 1) and discusses secular institutes (n. 11), proceeds on the whole according to a broad sense of "religious," which means, equivalently, "follower of the evangelical counsels in Church communities." The *Constitution on the Church,* in the chapter on the religious life, uses as its central conception the notion of three evangelical counsels, and says explicitly that "the faithful of Christ can bind themselves to the three . . . counsels *either* by vows, *or* by other sacred bonds which are like vows in their purpose" (n. 44).

It is interesting that the proposed norms for the revision of canon law submitted in 1968 by our American Conference of Major Superiors of Women, while they do preserve the distinction of religious institutes, societies of common life and secular institutes, do not speak of vows as proper to religious institutes. "Public profession of Christian life in community in the way of the Gospel counsels" is how permanent incorporation is described (n. 48).

Theologically speaking, I would say that the distinction between the three kinds of Church communities following the life of the counsels is of real but secondary importance. To make too much of this distinction runs the danger either of doing an injustice to the depth of consecration of members of secular institutes and societies of common life, or else the danger, in the name of separation from the world, of keeping apostolic religious men and women from the kind of life and contact with the world which their mission in the twentieth century calls for. Theologically, too, it is not of primary importance whether one refers to the permanent consecration as vow, promise, commitment, covenant, engagement. It is better to have a promise and keep it well than to have a vow and keep it badly.

A second question: How important is it that there be three vows or promises, and that these three have the names of poverty, chastity, and obedience? I would say it is not very important that the formulation of the consecration should be specified in this traditional way; the important thing is that the life itself be chosen and lived which corresponds to the traditional formula. History, of course, tells us of many changes and developments in the formula of consecration. The tradition of the East, the Benedictine rule, the fact that there was no general vow of obedience till about the ninth century, are some illustrations of this. This does not mean, obviously, that the realities designated by poverty, chastity and obedience are not part of the life of the counsels. It does mean that there are a variety of ways of conceptualizing this evangelical life. For example, one may conceive that celibate Christian community for the sake of the kingdom is the heart of the life, and that poverty, or the sharing of goods, and obedience derive their importance primarily from their value in fostering celibate community.

A third question: What is to be said on the subject of temporary vows? The *Instruction* of the Congregation of Religious on formation gives to the general chapter the power, by a two-thirds majority, to replace temporary vows with some other kind of commitment. My own feeling is that, whatever the value of temporary vows in the past, they present such difficulties for so many today that, generally speaking, they should be left behind. Undoubtedly different communities, on the basis of experience and reflection, will work out a variety of ways in which a member will be related to the community prior to her definitive commitment, and ways in which such relationships can be formulated and celebrated.

A fourth question concerns the time of life best suited to permanent commitment, and the length of time that should elapse between entrance and permanent commitment. The *Instruction* on Formation sets limits of three to nine years from the end of the novitiate. Here again experience and reflection should be the guide. There seems to be a growing consensus that the length of the period should be shaped to the individual, and the time of definitive consecration should be fixed by mutual agreement. There seems likewise to be agreement that, at least in general, definitive engagement to the religious life should not be undertaken before the middle or late twenties. Dr. Joseph English has suggested that the 20-to-30 period in the development of young people be creative and generative, not decisional.[1] This may pose practical

[1] Cf. *Celibacy: the Necessary Option* (ed. G. Frein), New York, 1968, p. 157.

problems, as for instance, with the ex-nun of 27 or 28 who enters into a rather competitive marriage market. And one wonders about the permanent commitment to marriage which in our society takes place usually at a time when the creative and generative period has hardly begun. In any case, the time to say "forever" and really mean it is the time when a relative maturity has been achieved, the time when a realistic appreciation, based on some appropriate experience of other possible options, makes the decision for this kind of life as fully free as possible.

We begin now to move toward the more basic questions. For example: can the religious life, in its essentials, be lived without a lifetime consecration to it, with the door always open, so to speak? Here again, it is important to keep in mind several distinct questions. I will be arguing later that the life of the counsels, as a distinct Christian life-form, does call for a permanent engagement. But there are several things which this permanent engagement does not exclude. First, it does not exclude that we have some groups or communities in the Church, including celibate groups, in which permanency of commitment is not part of the structure, in which the decision to remain celibate for the sake of apostolic work in a particular group will have the nature of a career decision fully open to be changed. Secondly, it does not exclude that, within a community whose basic or core membership is committed on the basis of a life-time dedication, there should also be associate members who never make such a life-time commitment. In the conditions of life today, there would seem to be a good deal to be said for such communities, which have historical antecedents in such kinds of membership as that of oblates and donnés.

A further question here would be whether such associate membership could be extended to married people. The various efforts made at heterogeneous communities (celibates and married) in the past are not entirely encouraging, but it may be that we are in a period of the life of the Church and the world where this difficult dream may be capable of realization. I would understand such a conception as being in continuity with the association that religious and seculars had in the past through Third Orders, sodalities and similar groups.

Even if one grants that such heterogeneous groups should now have a greater place in the Church, there is the further question whether they should not be, by and large, new groups. We all need to come closer to married Christians, but this can take place in various ways. Where the relationship would be so intimate as to involve proper membership, however, we have to ask whether the consequent adjustment of institutions and mentality would be truly creative or whether it would be destructive. Not every form of Christian living is for everyone. Our history provides us with opportunities, but they are not unlimited. "In my father's house there are many mansions," and, thank God, they are not all built to the same blueprint.

The final question is the most fundamental and difficult. It is the basic question of the legitimacy and special value of a lifetime consecration to God and man within the context of a particular celibate community. For many reasons—psychological, cultural, religious—this is a widespread doubt which has come into the minds of many today. Let me first explore some of the reasons for doubting, and then suggest a few avenues of theological and pastoral reflection.

First, this question stems in large part from massive cultural change. Permanency in the ancient and medieval world was one thing, permanency in the modern and contemporary context is another. The cosmos of ancient and medieval man invited men to prize permanency and stability. The stars were fixed in their places, or at least fixed in the regular cycle of their predetermined course. Everything had its natural place in the Aristotelian world, and should it be temporarily dislodged from its place, it was impelled by inner forces to get back to where it belonged. Such a view of the cosmos invited men to conceive the human microcosm, both individual and corporate, as being likewise a very orderly and static thing, in which sheer permanency was to be treasured. Everyone had his place in society, the king, the nobles, the commoners, the serfs. Economically, society had little mobility: if you were born a serf, chances are you would die a serf. And in the Church the various orders and states designated where each person and group belonged.

In such a world, permanency was a prime value. God's eternity tended to be conceived as the permanency of a God who never changed. If man's vocation was to be like God, then permanency was man's destiny, too, and stability in the forms of life the more appropriate way to reach the goal. Human life on earth would thus anticipate and reflect the unending and unchanging peace of the eternal city.

But now all has changed. From Darwin to Teilhard we have assimilated into our consciousness the feeling that nothing is permanently itself, that primate gets transformed into man; and man, we suspect, may well be destined for a transfiguration into something or someone we can't as yet imagine. Einstein has taught us that all things are relative. Marx has interpreted history as a dialectic, a struggle in which it is not just the same thing over and over again, but a movement to a goal which, though inevitable from one point of view, still has to be created, particularly by an avant-garde, a spearhead group. And Freud has involved us in the anxious quest for what we really are, for an understanding of what we really meant when we said, "Forever," and in the growing doubt that perhaps we really didn't mean it, really didn't say it freely, and that we now have to search elsewhere for our true identity. Kierkegaard has held up to us the ideal of the lonely knight of faith, forever in pursuit of the impossible dream. And currently we all seem to be in the throes of a binge of romanticism, with every man free to do his thing, usually a different thing, and a changing thing. These and many other influences have made our world one in which it is not permanency and stability which are honored, but mobility, process, pluralism of points of view, an accent on contingency, the spirit of search, and the refusal of total commitment lest we be trapped into a sterile and invalid existence. All of these are in the air we breathe today, and our young people have hardly breathed any other air at all. Kenneth Keniston speaks in his study of alienation among the young of "an unwillingness to make commitments that might seem to limit the capacity for experience." [2] In such a world, are perpetual vows not a closing of the door which leads to experience, life, adventure?

To these cultural reasons why permanency is in crisis today we must add some theological and religious ones. Historically it was Martin Luther who challenged the validity of a binding, lifetime consecration by vow, and he did so in the name of the Gospel. Monastic vows, he argued, were an insult to God and man: to God because they were a pretentious effort at justification by works, by human merits, an assault on the freedom of God to bestow his gifts on whom he will; an insult to man because they deprived Christian man of his freedom to respond to the Spirit wherever he might call.

There is, in Catholic circles today, a good deal of sympathy with this viewpoint of Luther on permanent vows, as on several other questions. By binding ourselves for life to a particular community, are we not unduly limiting our freedom to follow the call of the Spirit? The development of the theology of marriage and of secular engagement in the world has opened the eyes of many religious to alternative options for dedicated Christians, married or celibate. Especially if our community be reluctant to renew itself, how can there be a responsibility to stay with that foundering and possibly sinking ship till death, when life outside the community

[2] *The Uncommitted*, Delta, 1965, p. 192.

beckons us to a richer human and Christian experience, to a freer service of human needs, and perhaps to a more demanding responsibility to God and man.

Sometimes, in response to such objections, appeal is made to the permanency of the marriage covenant. Those who question the value of permanency in religious life will answer sometimes in terms of the needs of children which is peculiar to the marriage covenant, and sometimes more radically by saying that we have to rethink the permanency of marriage, too.

Finally, where the defenders of permanency stress the incomparable value of an absolute lifetime commitment to God, the doubters will respond that this covenant is not the prerogative of religious but the gift and responsibility of every baptized Christian. A religious who decides, even after many years, to carry out this commitment within marriage is changing only the form of his following of Christ, not the substance. *The* vocation is the baptismal vocation.

Such, in brief, are some of the reasons offered today in what can be described as a crisis of permanent consecration. When these intellectual arguments are confirmed by the withdrawal from religious life of large numbers of men and women, including some of the most talented, then we are all impelled to ask: What price permanency? Would it not be more Christian and more practical simply to relinquish the mystique of permanency in the religious consecration, make it easier for people to come and go, and assume a much simpler and less idealistic stance toward this form of Christian life?

I have no overall answer to the problem. I would like to suggest some approaches, especially of a theoretical kind, centering around the notion of fidelity. In many ways, the key to the problem of permanency is in the idea and the experience of fidelity, in its psychological, philosophical and theological dimensions.

Fidelity is, first of all, a value and a response consequent upon an experience of another person or of a community, an experience of that person or community in its mystery and in its exigency. At a particular moment of my personal history, my destiny has become intertwined with another destiny, and this moment of epiphany, of revelation, has brought into my life a joyful but compelling necessity which was not there before. *I can do no other*—this is the way Fr. Schillebeeckx expresses it. Not that I am not free to choose, either initially or afterward. I can do no other in the sense that once I have incorporated this meeting with the other into my way of identifying myself, I cut off, in some genuine sense, the possibility of living my life otherwise than as a response to this person or community.

This moment of discovery and my commitment to let it shape my life finds expression in the word, the promise, the vow. I am yours, you can depend on me, I will be there, I will be true to thee till death. And with the word, the pledge, the vow, the other person (or the community) can likewise let this moment of encounter shape his life. To the extent to which he trusts me and believes in my fidelity, he can make demands, and he can face his own future in hope because now it is a shared future.

I have given my word and I cannot take it back. Fidelity therefore has in it the quality of being closed, definite, once for all. Each word of ours has so many syllables, so many particular sounds, so many letters. So, too, the pledged word gives to fidelity an element of stability and permanence. I have paid my vow to the Lord and I cannot take it back. But the mystery of fidelity has in it also the opposite quality of being open. It is related to the unknown future as well as to the clear and definite past. Fidelity would be a mere pragmatic contract fulfillment if we knew fully in advance what it demands. When we give our word to another person or community, we are not making a cautious contract hedged in with safeguards and escape clauses. Rather we are saying, "I will be there no matter what." We are saying, "I take you for better or for worse, for richer or for poorer, in sickness and in health, until death."

And so fidelity is a paradox of the closed and the open, the fixed and definite and the indefinable. It points to the past but also to the future. Theologically, the mystery of Christian fidelity is rooted in the mystery of God, who speaks his Word and breathes forth his Spirit—his once-for-all Word, which stands forever, in Jesus Christ, the living Word of the Lord, and his Holy Spirit, who is love and breath and wind and fire, who comes from God only knows where and leads to God only knows where. In proportion as we share life with Father, Son and Spirit, we shall come to understand the meaning of Christian fidelity, and vice versa: living the mystery of Christian fidelity plunges us more and more into the mystery of Father, Son and Spirit.

Into every commitment of Christian fidelity must enter the note of *forever*, the quality of deathlessness. We can, of course, speak of fidelity to a promise to do something that is temporary—to make a pilgrimage or a novena. But when there is question of a basic life-option, of a profound reorientation of our life, as in marriage or consecration to God in celibate community, some element of the "forever" must be present, if we are to respect the meaning of such options. We are not talking about a mere career decision, not even a very important one; such decisions fall short of the kind of dedication envisaged by Christ and the Church in the call to follow the evangelical counsels. Here I have two observations to make:

1. When man says "forever" or "till death" as he engages himself in fidelity, he is not saying, "for a very long time." The "forever" is merely a very imperfect expression of the *depth*, the *quality* of his engagement. There is no special value in duration as such; it is valuable only to the extent to which it expresses or confirms the element of depth, intensity, quality in our love. Fifty years in the religious life are not

necessarily of more value than five years. A person who engages himself for one year with intensity and then dies or leaves for good reason has been far more faithful than someone who just sticks it out superficially for fifty or sixty years.

2. When a person says "till death" when he consecrates himself to God, he is not merely indicating the expiration date of a contract. He is rather prefiguring the event of his death in Christ as the consummation of his lifelong consecration. He wants so to live, so to anticipate that supreme moment, that it will be the most perfect act of covenant love. That is why he is willing, under vow, to live each day a death to some of life's most cherished values, so that his death itself, when it comes, may be the most perfect consecration for life. I do not think we can adequately appreciate Christian fidelity, or the meaning of a vowed existence, unless we relate it to death in Christ both in baptism, in daily Christian existence, and in the moment of passage from this world to the Father.

And so, I suggest, if there is a crisis regarding permanency in religious life today, it is ultimately a crisis of depth, a crisis of the quality of the commitment both in its initial moment and subsequently. Recently I heard a psychiatrist familiar with the religious life quoted as saying that, while we have taken steps to see that only well balanced people will enter religious life, we now need to be concerned lest we end up with superficial people, people without depth. Bernard Lonergan, in speaking of the capacity for autonomy as characteristic of the adult, writes very perceptively about the opposite quality: [3]

The opposite to this open-eyed, deliberate self-control is drifting. The drifter has not yet found himself; he has not yet discovered his own deed and so is content to do what everyone else is doing; he has not yet discovered his own

[3] "Existenz and Aggiornamento," in *Collection*, Herder & Herder: New York, 1967, p. 242.

will and so he is content to choose what everyone else is choosing; he has not yet discovered a mind of his own and so he is content to think and say what everyone else is thinking and saying; and the others too are apt to be drifters, each of them doing and choosing and thinking and saying what others happen to be doing, choosing, thinking, saying.

From Bernard Lonergan to the Beatles is quite a jump, but the Beatles, too, in their own inimitable way, have said (or sung) the same thing.[4]

NOWHERE MAN

He's a real nowhere man
Sitting in his nowhere land,
Making all his nowhere plans for nobody.

Doesn't have a point of view,
Knows not where he's going to.
Isn't he a bit like you and me?

Nowhere man, please listen.
You don't know what you're missin'.
Nowhere man, the world is at your command.

He's as blind as he can be,
Just sees what he wants to see.
Nowhere man, can you see me at all?

Nowhere man, don't worry.
Take your time; don't hurry.
Leave it all till somebody else lends you a hand.

Doesn't have a point of view,
Knows not where he's going to.
Isn't he a bit like you and me?

Nowhere man, please listen.
You don't know what you're missin'.
Nowhere man, the world is at your command.

He's a real nowhere man,
Sitting in his nowhere land,
Making all his nowhere plans for nobody.

At this point it would be quite comforting, for some of us at least, to use this idea of drifting, of the "Nowhere Man", to explain the large-scale departures from the religious life. Undoubtedly some who are leaving are people without depth, who in the pre-Vatican II Church were protected in their religious life by a favorable climate, stable structures, uniformity and regularity, but who now, in the new climate, find themselves without adequate personal resources to survive in the new and very exposed kind of existence.

But this is only one aspect of the total picture. I would suggest that when there is question of fidelity, of the depth and quality of consecration, in contrast to the spirit of drifting, we should ask the question also about our communities and about those who remain, and not only about those who leave. Could it possibly be that the reason why some individuals are leaving, individuals whose fidelity to Christ does have this quality of depth, is that their communities have substituted for genuine fidelity a dead conformity to the past, and, despite superficial reforms, are unable or unwilling to grow up in Christ, and so go on drifting and dreaming without substantive renewal?

What I am suggesting here is that the crisis of permanency is really a crisis of depth, a crisis of the quality of our covenant with the Lord. And if we wish really to come to terms with the problem of permanency, then all of us, individuals and communities, must face squarely the attitudes and conditions which make of us drifters instead of deeply committed Christians. Let us ask not only, "Are these individuals capable of a lifetime commitment?" Let us ask also, "Is this community able and willing to commit itself in covenant with the Lord unto death, i.e., with a depth and quality of commitment which corresponds to the depth and quality of the Spirit's call?" And am *I* able and willing for this *kind* of commitment? "Having loved his own who were in the world, he loved them to the uttermost limits of his love."

Mentioning the community in connection with fidelity prompts this further reflection: the covenant we make in the religious profession is a covenant with man and not only with God. When I say in the moment of ratifying this covenant, "I am yours," "I will be there," "You can depend on me," I am saying it to the members of my community (and more broadly to the whole Church and all mankind), and my community in turn is saying it to me. The day of religious profession is a day on which the community, along with its new members, professes its allegiance, its fidelity. On each profession day the whole community stands at the foot of Sinai, in the Temple, on Calvary, in a moment of covenant renewal.

This means, for example, that when an individual religious comes into a period of crisis and begins to reexamine his covenant—something which he not only may but sometimes must do—he has to ask himself not only, "How am I now to be faithful to my word pledged to the Lord?" but also, "How am I now to be faithful to my word pledged to my brothers and to the Church? I have told them as well as the Lord, 'You can depend on me,' and I must keep my word." This does not mean, of course, that fidelity will always keep a person in the community; it may in fact sometimes command that he leave. But the decision to leave, like the decision to enter, must be a decision taken, in some fashion, in the presence of the community, and not in isolation from it. And the community, on its part, must be concerned for its own fidelity to this individual member, not only in his entering and persevering, but also in his going, and, I would be inclined to say, after his departure.

But I have not yet touched on the most difficult aspects of our problem. What of the view that the only absolute commitment for a Christian is the one he makes at baptism, and that any further commitments must have a tentative character? I don't see how one can simply deny this. The basic consecration of every Christian is to love without limit, to follow the Spirit wherever he leads. And no Christian can have an absolute guarantee that God's baptismal call to him will continue till death to be a call to fulfill his baptismal promises within a celibate Christian community. To this extent Luther was right.

On the other hand, we cannot reduce the consecration to the life of the counsels merely to an important career decision which may be reversed with relative ease. The basic fact, verifiable in 2000 years of Christian history, is that Christ, who comes into the life of all Christians in varying degrees, comes into the life of some Christians in a distinctive way. It may be that these are people psychologically disposed for this special kind of call, that they are people whose revelatory experience with the mystery of life and death compels them to incorporate that mystery not only into their attitudes and responses to life but into the very structure of their life. From this point of view, celibacy, poverty, obedience are three exclamation points placed after the name of Christ Jesus at the head of the *curriculum vitae* of these Christians; they are a cry—at once a warning and an invitation and a song and a protest and a laugh—a cry addressed to anyone willing to open his ears, but also a cry that doesn't care whether anyone is listening at the moment or not.

Only love is credible, says Hans Urs von Balthasar, and this bridging of the credibility gap in contemporary life must be written not only into the substance of Christian living but into its form. This particular form of Christian living, the life of the counsels, unlike other forms, is itself incredible unless there is love. And I mean not merely, "Unless there is human love, unless human beings care for one another." I mean, "unless there be, at the very bottom of human life, underneath the pain and the pleasure, the discovery and the bafflement, the great hopes and the little despairs, at the very wellsprings of life, a love which surpasses all understanding, and which we call God."

Only love is credible, but perhaps this divine love, being so profound and hidden, needs itself to be rendered credible by the lives of those who believe that the first and the last word is God who is love; and perhaps this rendering of love credible, which is the work of faith, requires that in some Christian lives, at least, there be an unambiguous witness that it is love—divine love—that makes the world go round. To attach a date of expiration to such a witness, or to put it in the category of career choices, seems absurd. And once again, the issue is not permanency but quality: What kind of choice is the religious profession? If it is a choice in depth, a quality choice, if it is a congruous response of fidelity to him whose great love is without end, then it is hard to view it except as qualitatively different from ordinary career decisions.

I have no illusions about having plumbed the depths of explanation of the mystery of consecration for life, or about having answered the many difficulties, theoretical and practical, surrounding this mystery. What I have said may, however, enable us to say something about these difficulties. For example: the fidelity involved in consecration for life in the qualitative sense is not to be identified with the medieval prizing of permanency as such. Here let me refer to the pages in Sister Helen Marie Beha's book on the meaning of fidelity to commitment, and how it differs from mere constancy.[5]

What I have said may help, too, in understanding and evaluating departures from religious life. When the crisis arises,

---

[5] *Living Community*, Bruce: Milwaukee, 1967, pp. 32-49.

there are many questions which must be faced: Did the individual ever really make a permanent commitment in the qualitative sense? Did he enter a community which was itself able and willing to live at this intensity of life? Where the original commitment was truly free, we must try to see to it that, in the hour of crisis, the individual religious realizes that his commitment made him responsible to a community, and that the community now must enter into his reevaluation of commitment. We must try to see to it also that, as his original commitment was a loving response to the undying fidelity of God who is love, so now no change in the form of his life will take place except as a generous and discerning response to a relatively clear call of that same undying fidelity. And finally, because only God knows the hearts of men, both those who stay and sometimes appear mediocre, and those who leave and sometimes appear flighty or unfaithful, must remain for us what they are, our brothers and sisters, who need our compassion, and whose compassion we need.

In summary and conclusion, then: what is the meaning of consecration for life, fidelity unto death, in following the life of the counsels? What is its value and its justification? Here are some of the things we can say about it, and say for it: There are some people who find no other way of expressing and responding to the incredible love of God for men, and to the deathless fidelity of Jesus Christ to his beloved, the Church, except by writing the word "forever" with their own blood into the very shape and structure of their lives.

There are some people whom God calls to the gamble of faith, as Fr. Donald Heintschl has expressed it (and that word can also be spelled "gambol" and still be accurate and significant), because God asks them to entrust their weakness, their stupidity, to the weakness and stupidity of others like themselves, so that when the miracle of reconciliation and joy in community takes place, there can be no explanation except that the power and wisdom of God has appeared among us.

And there are some people whom God asks to make manifest in their life-style that human life is for pilgrimage and not for drifting; that our destiny is not to be "nowhere men" and "nowhere women" but a pilgrim people with roots in the City of God; that it is the quality and depth of human life which counts and not the number of years we live on this earth; and that the only congruous response for the gift of freedom is to give it back wholly to God, freedom's self and freedom's giver, without even the possibility, so far as in us lies, of ever again being free apart from him.

There are indeed such people, and religious are those people. If we glory in it—and I think we should—we do so not as some kind of elite (God knows we are not an elite!) but, like Paul, we glory that the power and wisdom of God has chosen our particular weakness and our unique stupidity to manifest itself to men, for the praise and glory of his grace.

Finally, does consecration for life in the way of the counsels have anything to say to contemporary man? Well, does contemporary man need a witness to fidelity? Does he need a reminder that his precious years on earth are given not for drifting but for pilgrimage? Does he need help to keep him from being a cipher, an anonymity, a "nowhere man"? Does he need to be called back to a taste and a yearning for quality and depth in human life? Can he be helped by seeing weak and foolish people like himself so willing to trust one another that they have promised one another to remain together until death? And does someone—perhaps relatively few, but still some—need to keep alive in the heart of contemporary man the embattled hope that behind the absurdity there is ultimate meaning, and beneath the carnage of death there is life, and that at the very end of the human pilgrimage there stands, still unseen and unheard, that one uncritical lover of man, that Father who entrusted his own Son to our human keeping, that Father who in Jesus Christ has loved us to the uttermost limits of love?

Franz Kafka left behind him, among his unfinished fragments, the vision of a vast city at night in which just a few people are awake. And he compared it to a military encampment in which everyone is asleep except a few guards on the battlements, keeping watch. And he asks why these few are awake when the rest are asleep. And he answers: "Because someone must be watching, someone must be there."

Perhaps, ultimately, this is all we religious can really say about ourselves when we speak of lifetime consecration; this is really all we can say about why we are here, in this stubborn and mischievous kind of life: because *someone* must be watching, *someone* must be there.

5

RESPONDING TO SECULARIZATION

How will religious respond to the ambivalence of con-
temporary society, which both supports and threatens person
and community? Pluralistically, as professionals, reformers,
radicals or "hippies."

Relevant renewal of the religious life will be achieved to
the degree to which religious communities of men and
women: (1) respond to the contemporary secular situation
(2) within the response of the contemporary Church (3) in
creative fidelity to the distinctive vocation of religious in
Church and world.

First, then, a relatively brief word on the contemporary
secular situation, especially in our own country. It may be
described in terms of the ambivalence of our present American society. This society has deep roots, to be sure, in the
Judeo-Christian and Greco-Roman heritage. More specifically, however, it is a society based on the great modern revolutions—intellectual, political, scientific and technological. It is,
quite obviously, a society in the throes of a crisis, a crisis that
is full of paradox. This society offers, on the one hand, the
promise and partial fulfillment of a better life for mankind,
but it also tragically poses a serious threat to the human person
and to genuine human community. The symbols of this ironic

cohabitation of human greatness and human degradation are all around us: hospitals where, thanks to science and technology, miracles of support for human life and health are performed daily, but where also an alarming shortage of personnel and of personal caring often makes them places of danger and anguish for human beings; our great cities, where towers of steel and glass adorn the skyline, but where also, in the very shadows of this splendor, children in tenements must learn to cope with rats and roaches. This roster of tragic contradictions could be indefinitely prolonged. These contradictions are raising today in the minds of many a question as to whether such a society can survive, whether it deserves to survive, whether it is worth the effort.

In this situation of crisis and ambivalence within secular life, one can discern, I think, four general reactions or tendencies, which sometimes intertwine. There is, first, an optimistic professionalism, which identifies with the existing order of things, and which is confident that present ills, however serious, are really growing pains in man's inevitable conquest of the good life, based on more science, more technology, and on the free processes of political democracy.

There is, secondly, reformism, which seeks within the present system to correct its inequities and to right its imbalances. Thirdly, there is radicalism, which calls for revolution of various degrees and kinds of violence, in order to replace the present system, which it judges corrupt beyond recall, with a new one. And finally, there is what I would call the "hippie" response or tendency, which by a conscious disengagement erects on the fringe of present society a protest, at once gentle and militant, on behalf of the person and personal community, on behalf of the celebration of life.

Such it seems to me, is the secular situation in which the Church and religious communities within the Church are living: a situation of crisis and ambivalence, eliciting these several responses. We might, perhaps too simply, express the secular problematic of our times somewhat as follows: Can our scientific, technological, liberal-democratic society effectively place its achievements and its vast potential at the service of the human person and of human community without, in the very process, decimating the human person and human community? What are the possible conditions for such a resolution of the present crisis? What contribution to such a resolution may we expect from each of the four tendencies I have noted?

These are crucial questions not only for the leaders of the secular society but for the men and women of the Church. Even though the Church brings to the secular something that is not derived from the secular, the credibility and effectiveness of her message will obviously be conditioned by the kind of world to which she addresses that message. And so I propose to speak now of the response of the Church to the contemporary secular crisis, under two headings: the nature of the challenge addressed to the Church; and some aspects of the Church's response.

The Church today lives in an autonomous secular society that developed, historically, in continuity with the Judeo-Christian tradition, but, tragically, also in opposition to the Church and with opposition from the Church. The relationship of the Church and society today is just the opposite of the medieval situation. At that period temporal institutions were subordinate agencies within a Christendom in which the clerical and monastic Church was the predominant influence. Today the Church exists as a still important but secondary element within an increasingly pluralistic and secular society; it is science and technology and their cultural corollaries that are the primary forces giving shape to human life.

The challenge to the Church resulting from this changed status is undoubtedly enormous and in some ways unique. This is not the first time, however, she has been called upon to make the passage from one culture to another. At the very

dawn of Christianity she was summoned to move out from
the land of her origins into the world of Greece and Rome.
Some centuries later the collapse of the ancient world brought
her the challenge not only of self-survival but of preserving
the heritage of ancient culture for the Western world. In the
Middle Ages she had to adjust to the transition from an agrar-
ian, feudal regime to life centered in the medieval towns. Always, in such periods of transition, there was need for profound adaptation of all Church institutions to the exigencies
of the new age.

And the challenge has always been to demonstrate, in
every sector of Church life—doctrine, liturgy, institutional
structure, existential forms of Christian living—that the Gospel
is viable in the new culture. We may take as symbol of this
perennial challenge the scene in Acts (16:9) where Paul, at
Troas, is confronted with a vision, the man of Macedonia who
stands and cries out to him: "Come over and help us." This is
really the way we might look, with the eyes of faith, on the
present challenge to the Church. Contemporary man, experiencing human life, for better or worse, in a way vastly
different from men of other ages, is in a hundred different
ways calling out: "Come over and help us." If the depth of
the challenge today is greater than in any previous period, so
is the opportunity. For today Macedonia is the whole of mankind, and the future of mankind on this earth is what is at
stake.

The tensions, doubts and tragedies that we are witnessing
are the expression of the radical readjustment that the contemporary Church feels called upon to make in response to
the present challenge. The challenge itself has been presented
in many ways: cosmocentrism versus anthropocentrism; a
metaphysical or classicist view of man versus an historical
one; the clash of a static outlook on man and the cosmos with
a dynamic—evolutionary and immanentist—one. In doctrine
the challenge is verified in a crisis of the demythologizing,

dedogmatizing, and relativizing of belief; in morality it takes the form of a confrontation between natural law based on eternal truths and an ethic of situation. It is concerned with the effort to respond to the critique of religion and Christianity made by Marx, Freud and others as being alienation and illusion. In its horizontal dimension it features a personalist and existentialist current strongly critical of hierarchical structures and established institutions.

The overall result is a climate of crisis that touches every area and aspect of the Christian life, and that in many cases is leading to the disengagement, more or less radical, of individuals and groups from the priesthood, from the religious life, from the Church itself. Even Christian belief, as doctrinal identity, is entering into a period of crisis in our American scene. The anti-institutionalism of the "underground church," which for a time gained both adherents and publicity, now leads more frequently to a more or less total disengagement. The vocation to celibacy for the sake of the kingdom is under fire. The young and the intellectuals, in large numbers, tend to become estranged from the main body of the Church Catholic. One cannot help but feel that what we are witnessing is a recurrence—within Roman Catholicism and compressed within the space of several years—of the same developments that took place in Reformation Christianity over a period of centuries.

If there is good reason to be sober in looking at the dimensions of the challenge confronting the Church today, there are also solid grounds for joy and hope when we turn to the response being made by the Church. We are probably too close to Vatican II to be able to appreciate fully what a remarkable achievement it was, not least as a response to the secular crisis of our day. Along with some of the encyclicals of Popes John and Paul, it has given us at least the main lines for a truly creative response to our times. *Gaudium et Spes,* for example, shows the Church coming to terms with the historical process of secularization by explicitly acknowledging the autonomy of the secular.

We find also in Vatican II and recent encyclicals a fresh realization by the Church of her mission in the secular order. What she now opens herself to is a dialogue-partnership with the secular on behalf of man—the human person and human community—or, to put it in the terms used by Pope John in *Pacem in Terris*, on behalf of an order grounded on truth, guided by justice, motivated by charity, realized in freedom, and flowering in peace. Here is where the heart of the Church's mission is to be found now. Here in the contemporary world is the Roman road opening the way for Christ and his Church to be significantly present to mankind where it is today—the struggle for man, for the whole man and the whole of mankind (as Pope Paul put it in the encyclical *On the Development of Peoples*), the struggle for the human person and human community, the effort to make this world a better world for all men.

But there are two important conditions for the success of this secular mission today. The Church must first of all remain herself; she must not be transformed into a merely secular agency, a political power. She has, of course, often been called on in history to stand in the breach when secular agencies fail or are nonexistent. But her distinctive contribution to the dialogue-partnership is not political or economic or cultural. Rather it is to be the sign and verification of the dimension of depth, transcendence and mystery in human life. In Henri de Lubac's striking epigram, quoted in *On The Development of Peoples* (n. 42): "Man can, indeed, organize the world without God, but only against himself."

Man needs God to be man; without God, man becomes a devourer of his fellow man: *homo homini lupus*. The presence of the Church to man's making of man is a necessity lest, without God, man destroy himself. In her very engagement within the secular—and I am taking it for granted that she

must be so engaged—she must keep a certain otherness, for the
sake of the world itself even more than for her own sake.
She is the Church *in* the world and *for* the world, but only
on condition that she not *be* the world. She betrays both herself and the world when she ceases to be herself, ceases to
challenge men to reach out for self-transcendence, to find
their destiny in the mystery of God.

Moreover, as the Church of Jesus Christ, formed by his
Spirit, her contribution to the secular is the paschal mystery,
the proclamation—by deed more than by word—that it is only
in self-transcendence and kenosis, whose paradigm is Christ
crucified and risen, that the human person and human community can really come into their own. However she may
need to adapt her message to the world of today, the Church
can never cease to be the bearer of the paschal mystery.

The second condition for the credibility and effectiveness
of the Church's secular mission is inner renewal and reform.
Unless the Church herself is a true home for the human person
and human community, her witness in the world on behalf
of person and community will be an empty word. How can a
Church where truth is not loved and practiced, especially at
the highest level, bear witness to truth in the world? How can
a Church, in whose leaders there does not burn a passion for
justice and freedom within the Church, profess without hypocrisy to champion the cause of justice and freedom in the
world? And how can a Church which cannot effectively promote the reconciliation of different temperaments and viewpoints within herself be a force for the reconciliation and
peace of mankind? Is it not her claim to be, at least in some
frail and inchoative way, Resurrection City, a challenge and
harbinger of how men may one day realize peace on earth?
The world today is looking to see if the Church today can
make good on that claim. This is the link between the out-
ward and inward aspects of Vatican II. Inner renewal and
reform are an absolute imperative for the witness and service
that the Church wishes to bring to the world of today.

One last word on the Church before coming to speak of religious. Because she is catholic, because she does not identify absolutely with any one culture or faction, she is able to perceive values present in all four of the current tendencies of which I have spoken: professionalism, reformism, radicalism and the "hippie" movement. Let others, if they wish, take a narrow, absolutizing and denunciatory stance toward one or other of these tendencies. The Church, like her Lord, is on earth to reconcile, not to denounce or condemn, to be the servant of the Spirit as he creates, out of our poor, stupid humanity, the future of man, the Christ that is to be.

We come, finally, to speak of the share of religious in the Church's mission in the secular on behalf of the human person and human community. At this stage of the Church's life, there should be no question but that religious have a place in this mission, that they must be present to the great human task of building the city of man. What I have said of the Church's secular mission, of the conditions of its credibility and effectiveness, must also be said of the share of religious in that mission.

First, the mission of religious in the secular will be effective and credible only on condition that, as religious, they remain what they are: basically and universally this means *celibate Christian community.* For particular orders and congregations it requires that they remain what they are within a particular tradition, stemming from a charismatic founder and enriching the life of the Church and the world with a diversity of charisms. There may be and should be discontinuity as well as continuity in this relationship to the past. I realize, too, that a particular way of life of a religious community can cease to have meaning and value in the ongoing life of the Church and so should be allowed and even encouraged to disappear. But until a clear sign of this is given, fidelity to historical charism is an imperative.

Secondly, the inner renewal and reform of our religious communities is an imperative if we are ever to give effective service and credible witness on behalf of the human person and human community. This helps us, I think, to specify the goals of reforms: it is not just updating structures, not just a general renewal of fervor; it is making the religious community a place where human beings grow as persons, and where persons live together in genuine human community; it is the creation, on a small scale, indeed, but in the sight of men, of an order of life grounded on truth, guided by justice, motivated by charity, realized in freedom and flowering in peace. The vision of *Pacem in Terris* is a vision for the Church, for the religious life, as well as for the world.

But, granted that they remain committed to celibate community, and that they must seek to reform their communities so as to promote the human person and human community, where are religious to take their stand in the society of today? How are they to present themselves to their contemporaries? What is to be their self-image? Are they professionals? Or reformers? Or radicals? Or Christian "hippies"? My suggestion is that both history and the very nature of the religious life manifest an affinity with all four of these stances, sometimes in combination, and that all four must be given serious consideration in the important options religious are being asked to make today. Let me explain this a little.

First, in the changing life of the Church, religious men and women have very often functioned as professionals, as the Church's civil service, so to speak. Today there is a deep running current of professionalism among many religious, a self-image that portrays the religious as a professional man or woman. There is also a widespread feeling that religious communities have much to learn from American professionalism, teamwork, management skills, and other important secular techniques.

This self-image of religious as professionals accounts, at least in part, for a certain secularizing tendency at work among religious. This tendency is bringing new tensions. The professional person tends to emerge as much more of an individual, and this places a strain on life in community, at least as we have understood community in the past. Nevertheless the tendency is itself quite legitimate, and even appropriate, for our present situation. It is no small thing that we have over 200,000 Americans, Christian men and women, who have dedicated themselves to a lifelong full-time service of the needs of their fellow men, and to the struggle for a better life for man on earth. Simply as a potential of professionalism, the religious communities of our country are of enormous significance.

Secondly, religious have also, especially in times of major renewal, constituted powerful *reform* movements within the *ecclesia semper reformanda*. One thinks particularly of the Dominican and Franciscan origins of the thirteenth century. Today many religious are in the forefront of reform movements within the Church and within secular society. This too is especially congruous with the nature of the religious life. The reformer's work is powerfully enhanced when his own personal willingness to risk all, to sacrifice, is manifest, and when it is clear that he is not looking for personal advantage. Religious are among those men and women in the Church whose sensitivity to the presence of evil in the Church and in the world is such that nothing less than a full-time, all-out effort to reform and renew human and Christian life will do. Like Francis of Assisi, Christ confronts everyone whom he calls to this life with the vision of his crumbling Church, and challenges him to rebuild it.

Thirdly, *radicalism* is of the very essence of religious life. The renunciation of domesticity inherent in the life of the counsels puts the man committed to the counsels in the stance of the radical. For the radical is, par excellence, the man who calls the status quo into question, the man who has staked everything, not on the present, but on the future, which he promotes with urgency. Who then deserves the name of radical or revolutionary more than the man who has heard the call of the kingdom and who can do no other than commit himself totally to promote the coming of the kingdom? But if this is true, if religious community represents Christian radicalism, then I ask if religious, particularly in America, have not in large part succumbed to a certain domestication that has deprived their lives and witness of the power of radical Christianity. As our living conditions, social status and outlook achieve the image, at least, of middle-class respectability, does our living of the counsels not become flabby and unimpressive? Is there not something pitiful and contradictory about comfortable celibates, shielded from the implications of their profession by stale routine and insidious custom? And is there not now emerging, in the dallying of some young and not so young religious with the so-called third way, a further danger of domestication, which will further deprive the radical witness of celibacy of its power to challenge the present for the sake of the future? Eschatologism is of the essence of the Christian faith. Once we stop straining forward to meet the future Christ in his coming we lose something of the spirit of Christ. The religious life has always been conceived as a special locus of this passion for the future. Today this eschatologism needs perhaps to put more stress on the continuity of world and kingdom than it did in the past. But it would be tragic if, in the name of professionalism or personalism, this explosive radical force for the life of the Church and of the world were to be rendered impotent.

Finally, it is no idle fantasy to speak of religious men and women, especially, perhaps, in the monastic tradition, as Christ's "hippies," as people who are "doing their thing," people who refuse to answer to the utilitarian norms of contemporary life, people who are involved in the celebration of life, dancing before the ark and asserting the primacy of the human person and of human community. Implicit, at least, in the monastic tradition, is this spirit of freedom in the face of human society, when that society tends to be flat, demonic, bourgeois and repressive, as our American society has largely become today.

This "hippie" spirit exists on both sides of the monastery wall today. Within the Church and within the religious life, an assertive spirit of freedom is protesting against conformism, institutionalism. Our young religious want to be free, as religious, as students, as apostolic men and women, as persons, to do their thing, to take their own unique risks in their own unique way, to set the conditions for their own personal growth and for the creation of forms of authentic human community that is not to be had just by following the rules of the game.

My own personal view is that this fourth tendency, too, like the others, has something to say to us. Let us think twice before we denounce it. Let us remember what Francis of Assisi and Ignatius of Loyola looked like to many of their contemporaries. And let us try, at least, to feel in our bones, or at least to experience intellectually, the anguish of the thousands today for whom the American way of life—as Hollywood, as Madison Avenue, as the man in the grey flannel suit, as gradualism in social justice, as massive economic processes destructive of beauty and freedom—appears as simply monstrous. Is it not ironic that just at the point where American Catholics have come to terms with liberal, progressive, pluralistic society, where they follow the rules of the game, mute their protest against pornography, for example, lest they seem guilty of a celibate over-preoccupation with it, precisely now other voices are crying out in protest on behalf of the human person and human community? Is there no significant role that some of us, at least, can play in this sector of the American battlefront?

Let me try now to sum up. I have been suggesting, first of all, that for a relevant renewal of religious life today we must succeed in situating our life and mission as religious within the life and mission of the Church as she responds to the contemporary secular crisis. This crisis, I have proposed, is one of ambivalence: the human person, human community is both fostered and endangered by our scientific, technological, democratic society.

I have outlined four current stances, and have suggested that both the Church and religious within the Church can legitimately associate themselves with all four of these stances, always, however, with a view toward defending and fostering the human person and his freedom and promoting human community. I have indicated two conditions of credibility and effectiveness in this historic mission of the Church and of religious on behalf of person and community: First, that the Church herself and religious remain what they are, the presence of the transcendent, the absolute, within the world of men, the abiding presence of Christ as the paschal mystery, the servant who was crucified that he might become the Lord who is risen indeed. And secondly, that through inner renewal and reform the Church and religious communities themselves become what they wish the world to be, a safe haven for the human person, a congenial home for human community.

It is rather common for us today to say that religious are and must be like Abraham, who, the epistle to the Hebrews tells us (11:8), went out at the call of God without knowing just where he was going. This beautiful description of the faith and hope of Abraham, our father in faith, surely is verified in us today: we do not know where we are going. We do not know what particular forms religious life will take in the Church tomorrow. We cannot even demonstrate that there will be a religious life in the Church tomorrow. But I am personally and fully convinced that our world today needs the religious life. I would describe that life as a celibate Christian community, consecrating, witnessing and giving service —on behalf of the human person, on behalf of the human community—through a distinctive living of the paschal mystery.

6

A MATTER OF STYLES

How can we respond to polarization between "charismatic" and "secular" styles among religious? And how do we deal with the paradox that religious historically have appeared as both an avant-garde and a body of civil servants in the Church? Here again, a certain pluralism is inescapable.

How many times have I heard religious comment, usually with a laugh, on the variety of types (and even of "characters") who seem called to this life. In the past few years, I have been struck by two interesting contrasts which I would like to describe. One has to do primarily with styles of personal faith. The second is more concerned with roles, even though, obviously, roles of different kinds are filled by persons of different kinds.

Charismatics and seculars

One of the more striking and important features in the life of post-Vatican II American Catholicism is the presence of two very different moods and styles regarding faith, prayer and the experience of God.

The first mood finds its most interesting form in Catholic

pentecostalism, or what many today prefer to call the charismatic revival. Here are some of its features. It speaks very readily to God, and of him. It finds it easy to believe that God speaks to us, and that he is present in our midst through his Spirit. It rejoices to read scripture, to celebrate the eucharist, to sing and pray, especially with the prayer of praise and thanksgiving and the prayer of petition. It believes that God sends the sunshine and the rain, and that his children should ask him for what they need or want.

This style of religious experience lives very comfortably within the institutional Church and works well with traditional forms and formulations. It is for reform, renewal, change —for what I am here describing is not a rigid Catholicism unwilling to change—but it makes it quite clear that traditional *values* are not expendable, however detached we may be regarding traditional *expressions* of these values.

The dominant mood of this first style is one of joy, gratitude, optimism, hope. It has no qualms about being religious and Roman Catholic, no hesitancy about the need for contemplation. Its language is positive, vibrant, "charismatic." Though deeply convinced that a genuine Christian spirit must show itself in deeds of love, it does not concretely give primacy to direct participation in the various political and social movements concerned for peace and justice.

The second style, in contrast, is more reluctant to speak *of* God, and probably addresses itself less frequently *to* God in a formal way. For it, prayer is not to be conceived as a speaking to God in any ordinary sense. Intellectually, the later Bonhoeffer, especially as mediated through Bishop John Robinson (remember?) and the earlier Harvey Cox, as well as the "death of God" theologians, have had considerable influence on Roman Catholics drawn to this style. To speak readily of and to God and Jesus Christ in an era of such monstrous inhumanity strikes it as almost indecent. It cultivates at least a relative and economic silence regarding the presence of Christ in our midst. "I can no more speak to Jesus Christ," I have heard a young sister say, "than I can speak to George Washington."

The adherents of this style prefer a language more open to tentativeness, doubt, pragmatism than that of the first style. They are also more willing to be critical of and detached from official Catholicism, its dogma, liturgical practices, discipline. One of the verifications of this tendency is what Daniel Callahan has termed the "unCatholic." It identifies more readily, in the name of the Gospel, with controversial political and social positions, and desires the Church and her leaders to do the same.

The dominant mood of this second style is one of honesty, modesty of aspiration, detachment from traditional forms and formulations, and a faith which cultivates an eloquent silence.

This brief description of the two tendencies fails, I realize, to do justice to complexity. Under almost every contrast I have made, one would have to make distinctions. And many blends, variations and waverings between the two are possible. A man like Daniel Berrigan shares much of both moods. Yet the broad comparison would appear useful and not entirely inaccurate. If so, it presents us with some important questions.

Do the two styles belong in the same Church? Can it be said, without hypocrisy, that they really share the same faith? Doesn't truth compel an acknowledgment that the gap here is not one merely of culture or psychology but of Christian substance?

In trying to respond to these questions our first responsibility is to accept them as real questions. A bland tolerance which excludes a priori the very possibility of heresy or schism is far from being Christian. The original sense of Augustine's oft quoted "Love [he meant love of neighbor] and do what you will," is that genuine love leads sometimes to disagreeing with and even chastising the Christian brother who is stubborn or in error. One of the interesting and hopeful signs of health today is the growing acknowledgment, influenced by the philosophy of nonviolent resistance, that the basic Christian will to unity and peace does not exclude but rather calls for tentative mutual challenges and conflicts with a view to dissolving false harmonies and evasive truces.

I am inclined to think, nevertheless, from contact with those who follow each style, that neither represents a distortion of the Gospel, even though each can be used as a "cop-out" from the hard demands of Christian discipleship. In the light both of Christian history, with its remarkable panoply of styles and moods, and of the contemporary need to search for new styles, there is no escape from pluralism.

What I would like to see develop in the American Church in general (what I am suggesting has been taking place, for example, in many religious communities and among diocesan priests) is an imaginative series of gatherings where outstanding exponents of each style could come together, to discuss, to argue, to challenge, but also and especially to pray and worship. I realize that *how* to pray, and even *whether* to do so, is itself a potential point of discord. But my hope would be that the faith of the participants, however different its favorite expression, would give them courage, freedom and trust to walk a mile or so with the brother in *his* direction, at *his* pace, and to speak to God or be silent about God in the style of the other before coming to any critical judgment about it.

All of this implies, of course, human and Christian maturity. To grow as a Christian is to grow in the ability to leave, at least on occasion, one's own style of religious experience, simply because one wants to share the style of another in whom he recognizes, beyond all superficial differences, a brother in Christ.

Consoling God-talk or sober silence, organ or guitar or nothing at all, the language of pentecostalism or of secularity —all this is important, and it is part of Christian maturity to recognize that one has limitations regarding religious experience. But in another sense, all this is not important. Like the man said: "What matters is not whether you are circumcised or not, but a new creation."

Avant-garde or civil servants?

Some are in parochial schools and some are in jail. Some staff hospitals and some picket. Some give assurance and some disturb. All are religious, men and women under vows. Given such striking contrasts, one cannot be blamed for asking: "What is the religious life all about? What are religious called to be?"

Once, in a seminary class on the different situations of people in the Church, I was asked by an especially perceptive Jesuit scholastic just who I thought were the secular counterparts of religious. Who fulfills in secular society the role or roles more or less analogous to those filled in the Church by religious?

The question is an important one. The rest of the Church, for one thing, needs to have a sound grasp of what it can reasonably expect from those whom it supports and on whom it relies in so many ways. If mothers and fathers are expected to encourage their children to think of religious life as a possible way of serving God and humanity, their image of what kind of people these sons and daughters will be should be undistorted. The young people themselves will suffer if they give themselves to this demanding form of life only to find that their basic expectation was a false one. And religious communities had better know what they are all about, not least if they are to invite others to join them in their distinctive way of seeking the Kingdom.

I answered the question—too quickly, I now see—by saying that the secular equivalents of religious are the artists, the

philosophers, the *avant-garde*, the critics of the establishment
—even the drop-outs and the hippies, people who are on the
fringe of society, challenging, warning, protesting, denouncing the status quo, calling radically for a better future for
man.

A fairly good case can be made, on the basis of history,
for this avant-garde image of religious. But my answer was
too facile because it failed to respect a certain paradox in the
vocation of religious. History testifies not only to the pioneering and sometimes gadfly character of religious communities, particularly in the period of their origins, but also
to the fact that they have been, in effect, the core of the
Church's civil service. If bishops and priests have been the
elected (or rather, appointed) official leadership, religious
have been like so many cadres of civil servants, part of the
institution, faithfully serving the leadership echelon and so
serving the whole Church.

This has been the case in a special way on the American
scene. If the predominant and distinctive image of American
Catholicism has been found in our parochial school system
and, to a lesser extent, in the vast system of hospitals and
other health care institutions, we have to thank religious
women.

This raises a rather serious question, especially in the context of the present tensions being experienced by religious
women within their own communities and in relationships
with the rest of the Church. Is it possible to put these two
characteristics, the adventurous spirit of the pioneer and the
prosaic devotion of the civil servant, together in the same
persons and communities, in the same life-style, except by
mere juxtaposition and at the price of intolerable tensions
and antinomies?

I am inclined to think that it is possible and indeed very
necessary, if religious life is to embody the spirit of the
gospel. Hugo Rahner has summed up a basic characteristic

of true mysticism in the Ignatian phrase *caritas discreta* (discerning love), i.e., the ability and willingness to situate the fire of one's inner vision within the uninspiring structures of institutional Christianity.

If charity is the flame without which institutions and structures are dead men's bones, discretion or prudence is the moderating and mediating factor that keeps the flame from destroying what it is called to illumine and warm. Charism and institution are both integral to being a religious community. A particular individual or group may be called to accent one or the other, and there needs to be something of mutual challenge and correction. But neither is simply dispensable. The image is a difficult one, to be sure, but religious are, in the final analysis, avant-garde civil servants, situated at the radical center. With God all things are possible, and usually rather exciting.

Some great historian has pointed out a significant difference between Roman Catholicism and Protestantism. In the former, the religious orders and congregations have provided ways *within* the Church in which radical Christians could channel their torrential enthusiasm. In Protestantism, on the other hand, the more typical phenomenon has been the breaking off of radical Christians from the more prosaic larger bodies to form sects.

Whatever the validity of the comparison, history does seem to disclose that religious serve as both challenge and support to the institutional Church. By the very fact that a Christian chooses to step out of the long line leading to marriage and family, he raises questions in people's minds. The history of religious life is filled with stories of opposition to charismatic beginnings on the part of family, secular authority and Church dignitaries. And yet we find, built into the charism of the pioneers, a deep devotion to the Church, a desire to be at the service of "ordinary" Christians, especially if they are needy, and a willingness to put up with the mediocrity, sometimes scandalous, to which all bureaucracy is prone.

Then, too, the religious community, however charismatic its origin, must eventually institutionalize itself if it is to be rugged enough to withstand the erosions of time and cultural change. It needs its own formal structures and processes. And if it is to serve in the real, everyday Church, it must learn to reckon with (which is not the same as to capitulate to) the power structure and the sedentary element in official Church life.

Nevertheless, at the present juncture, it is the avant-garde character of religious life that needs accenting. By comparison with other lay Christians (and religious as such have not left the ranks of the *laici*), religious are called to signalize by their lives that mankind must not settle down, but constantly strain forward toward the goal of history which transcends family, politics, economics, culture. And by comparison with the clergy, who are called to represent the Church and Christ in an official way in which religious are not, the latter retain an autonomy and mobility of apostolic witness and service that are not possible for the official leaders.

In addition to these theological considerations, there are some contingencies of history which would seem to call for a present accent on the radical nature of religious life. Religious in the past have often been asked to function as a kind of semiclerical cadre. Laymen have generally looked to them for a subtle kind of spiritual assurance, the price of which was that the "good nuns" did not effectively challenge some of the un-Christian religious and moral attitudes of the "good Catholic laymen" whom they served so well in school and hospital. For a while, at least, there is a certain amount of "shaking up" of the rest of the Church by religious that is not only inevitable but highly desirable. For, in final analysis, it is the entire Church, not merely religious, that is called to *caritas discreta*, to a paradoxical tension between charism and institution, between challenging humanity and serving its needs. Religious really succeed in their vocation when they function not as substitutes but as representatives, when they evoke from all in the Church a deeper realization that to be Christian is to be part of a pilgrim people.

And so, while I have not felt that my own personal call was to invade draft offices or to denounce the ecclesiastical establishment, and while I sometimes am impatient or nervous when others feel so called, I am glad of at least one effect of such efforts on the part of some of my brothers and sisters. They are dramatically manifesting that, while most religious may be called to the quiet courage of unsensational daily self-sacrifice as part of the Church's civil service, no religious can escape the call to strenuous and risky discipleship. Whatever good reasons may exist for following this vocation, they do not, especially today, include a wistful yearning to be "where the green swell is in the havens dumb/ And out of the swing of the sea."

7

POVERTY: WITNESS
AND INVOLVEMENT

*Professional service of the poor, without a personal presence
which seeks a share in their privation, does not measure up
to the exigencies of evangelical poverty.*

When I think of the poverty of religious today, I think
instinctively of two well-known Christian women (neither
of them "religious") who have, in quite different ways, dedicated their lives to the service of the poor. One is Dorothy
Day, founder and, for about forty years, leader of the Catholic Worker movement. The other is Barbara Ward (Lady
Jackson), world-famous economist and writer. However similar in many respects, these two figures present, for purposes
of the present reflection, a relevant contrast.

What is characteristic of Dorothy Day's service of the poor?
I think we may describe this way as one of personal involvement with poverty and with the poor in the ordinary material
sense. For years she has lived with the poor, on the Bowery,
in Chinatown and elsewhere, offering hospitality, food, shelter,
clothing to whoever has come. Her extensive travels have
usually been by bus. Her dress has been that of a poor woman.
She has been in jail and has personally experienced the deg-

radation of womanhood that often occurs in such places. With due respect to her talents as speaker and writer, it seems safe to say that the enormous influence she has exerted in drawing others to serve the poor has been exercised primarily by way of personal involvement, through the witness of literal poverty.

In contrast, Barbara Ward's witness to the need of concern for the poor has been expressed, at least in its social impact, primarily through professionalism. Through her services as economic consultant in underdeveloped countries, and especially through the eloquent and challenging exposures in her lectures and writings of the increasing gap between rich and poor nations, she has sought to stir the public conscience to deal effectively with this massive injustice of the contemporary world. The expertise of persons and organizations, the material resources of whole nations, the economic and political processes of a growingly complex world—these have been the target of her dedicated concern.

I have selected these two women, not because they are not religious (though there is food for thought in this fact) but largely because of their fame. For Dorothy Day I could have substituted, perhaps, Mother Teresa in India; for Barbara Ward, one of a growing number of religious women who have taken posts in government or other secular agencies working on behalf of the poor. But it is the contrast itself that concerns me most. It gives rise to the question: To what extent can the poverty of religious men and women be separated from personal presence to the literally poor, from personal experience of material privation? Is it possible and even necessary, within an affluent society, to reconceptualize the gospel counsel of poverty in such a way that such direct involvement and experience are no longer considered essential? Should we religious simply acquiesce in a situation which is very real for a good many religious today, namely, a material existence which economically and sociologically belongs to the middle class and even to the upper middle class?

If the members of a particular religious community live in expensive houses (I have seen parish convents for fifteen to twenty sisters built at the cost of two or three hundred thousand dollars), sit down to comfortable meals prepared and served by hired servants, have available the best of medical and psychiatric care, are put in private hospital rooms when sick, and have their needs in clothing and recreation taken care of according to the standards of a middle-class existence, is such a life in basic continuity with the life of gospel poverty as lived by religious down the centuries? If so, how is the rationale of gospel poverty to be described theologically? Should one speak of a spiritual poverty according to a concept so broad that a religious giving of his time and talents generously and in a professional way is following the counsel of poverty, even though his style of material existence is quite comfortable? Many today are inclined to think so. Others, despairing of the possibility of combining effective professional service of the poor with a full sharing of the condition of the poor, are suggesting that we stop using the term poverty to describe a life which is not itself poor in the ordinary sense, and which is actually intended to reduce and even eliminate the poverty of other men. Some few religious, perhaps, such as Mother Teresa, will be called to literal poverty; but the great majority of us must renounce any romantic conception of being poor with Christ, recognize the very real abnegation demanded by professionalism and availability, and accept the security and comfort normally required by people of the professional class. It is not in poverty, many feel, but in consecrated celibacy, or in commitment to community, that the center of the religious life must be sought.

I am not sure whether my answer to this dilemma is a good one. In any case I do not envisage it as *the* answer, and probably we cannot look for any definitive answer, even in that relative sense in which Christian mystery admits of such. Perhaps I can help myself and others to seek an answer by first asking the question: How do we go about seeking an answer? Practically every treatment which I have seen of the contemporary problem of religious poverty is concerned exclusively with the content of question and answer, not with the hermeneutical problem involved. Perhaps we need to look into the assumptions of the various views put forth, and see whether such assumptions are not leading us on a wild goose chase. And then we might ask positively how we ought to go about identifying the counsel of poverty in our own day. Only then may it be possible to sketch, in a very tentative manner, its principal features, and to distinguish what is historically conditioned from what is enduring.

One of the hidden assumptions we have to question is that the counsel of poverty is a clearly delineated essence, established once for all, against which each concrete verification must be measured. This making of a thing out of an attitude, of a complexus of relationships, of a human situation, needs to be challenged. There is, in fact, no such *thing* as a counsel of Christian poverty. Poverty is not a thing, a substance, which can be analyzed or dissected or put through a filter to separate cultural sediment from pure gospel essence. There is only God and his Christ, on the one hand, and ourselves on the other. There are our relationships, our attitudes, our situation. These are quite varied, even among Christians, and even among those who have been called "religious." These relationships, attitudes, and situations include among their many elements the material world and man's relationship to it. But the poverty to which some Christians are called is not a codified essence with particular forms hanging on it like baubles on a Christmas tree. It is historically identifiable, but not abstractly definable. It is capable only of partially adequate conceptualization. Only existentially, through discernment, can it be judged whether a particular form of life is in basic continuity with the historic reality of the counsel of gospel poverty.

A second working assumption which must be questioned is

that the meaning of the poverty of religious can be understood in isolation from other aspects of their life. When mere
juxtaposition, instead of a dynamic organic interaction, is
characteristic of our approach to the different facets of the
one life of the counsels, an inevitable impoverishment and
even distortion results. It may be necessary, for purposes of
analysis, to make partial and tentative precisions in dealing
with a mystery whose rational understanding involves complexity. But one cannot speak of poverty with even a minimal
adequacy without relating it to community, to celibacy and
obedience, to the element of consecration to God, to apostolic
witness and service.

A third assumption, or at least tendency, has been to deal
with the life and holiness of religious as if it were qualitatively different, precisely as a life, from that of other baptized Christians; as if the radical character of the gospel
message were addressed only to some Christians, and not to
all. Fortunately, we are moving away from this tendency
today. The *situation* of religious, from both a simply human
and from a distinctively Christian point of view, does differ
qualitatively, I would say, from that of the married Christian:
the free renunciation of marriage and parenthood is a basic
option which reaches down to the roots of personality and
thus radically specifies his life-situation. But the *life* of the
religious remains the same life as that of other Christians:
faith, hope and love. While we cannot here go into the difficult question of commandment and counsel, the framework
of our reflection on the poverty of religious is the call of
all men to live in the spirit of the counsels.

Having excluded certain misleading assumptions, it may
now be possible in a more positive way to indicate the road
we are to travel in judging what forms, practices and attitudes are today compatible with (that is, in basic historical
continuity with) the counsel of poverty as lived by religious.
I would here suggest two words as pointing to the necessary

methodology: discernment and congruity. By discernment I mean a judgment which, while dependent on empirical data drawn from history and from contemporary human life, as well as on rational analysis, is ultimately intuitive, a gift from the Spirit which is at the same time a call. This discernment of the call of the Spirit here and now will include as a primary ingredient a certain sense of congruity. The compatibility or the opposite of certain forms with the total reality and meaning of the life of the counsels lived in ecclesial community, will be judged in terms of a certain feeling for what fits, for what is appropriate and compatible, from the viewpoint of psychology, sociology, economics, culture, and especially, of course, faith.

Perhaps I can illustrate this rather abstract guideline with the help of history. At certain periods in the life of the Church, the Spirit moved certain people, who were often saints, to innovate and adapt. Ignatius Loyola in his desire of having religious priests not bound to choir, Francis de Sales and Vincent de Paul in their vision of apostolic religious women free to leave the cloister to serve the neighbor, are some notable examples. Until these saints raised their challenging questions, certain assumptions regarding the concrete identity of the life of the counsels were taken for granted. The raising of the questions provoked opposition, some of it rather effective, at least for a time. Ultimately the Spirit moved the Church to see that the form of life to which these saints and their followers were called was in basic continuity with the life of the counsels as lived for centuries in the Church. A true development of understanding had been achieved. It was now clearly seen, as it had not been previously, that, for example, ecclesial community of the counsels was quite compatible with a life outside the narrow confines of the cloister for dedicated Christian women.

More than one reader may by now have given up finding anything in this article which will help him to understand the poverty of religious better. But, unless we understand the question we are asking, and have some idea of how an answer is to be sought, we will continue to go round and round, saying some valuable things, without doubt, but never arriving at satisfactory answers to our urgent practical questions regarding poverty. And what I have said is a long preliminary to what I now propose to do: namely, reexamine in outline the elements traditionally associated with poverty, to see, if possible, which elements are so important for it that to eliminate them would create a life-form in discontinuity with the historical reality of religious life. For the theologian, the challenge here is so to organize the aspects of poverty, as well as the relationship of poverty to other aspects of the religious life, that a certain harmony or congruity appears, and one can see how there is mutual interdependence and support among all the elements. This is a theological task which proceeds not primarily by deduction or induction or rational analysis of concepts, but by a kind of quasi-esthetic sense able to relate the multiple dimensions of a single organic reality.

Before trying to identify poverty in its basic elements and to relate these elements among themselves, I must first try to do the same for the religious life in general. I do this with a minimum of embellishment and without argumentation. Most of the conceptions are familiar to the reader from recent discussions. I conceive the religious life, then, as:

1. An embodiment of Christian faith, hope and love. (In this it does not differ from the life of other Christians);

2. expressed in a basic life-option and life-situation aimed at portraying dramatically the exigencies of Christian discipleship, the mystery of the cross and resurrection, the primacy of the kingdom of heaven, of grace, of God and of the transcendence of human destiny;

3. this dramatization of the gospel message is for the sake of the salvation of all men;

4. and takes place within a community of faith, that is, a community not founded on blood (the family) or on merely natural affinity or friendship or functional utility (the typical secular organization), but only on faith and hope in the power of God to bring life through death;

5. simultaneously, this life-option and life-situation represents a special consecration to God and to Jesus Christ, who, through contemplative prayer, is apprehended as loving and beloved:

6. this dramatic consecration and embodiment of Christian faith, hope and love, considered as a basic life-situation, is integral in character: that is, it includes the special consecration of human freedom through obedience, in which the lifelong sharing of decision with the community is the vehicle of radical and total obedience to God; the special consecration of human affection, in which the lifelong mutual love for the members of the community assumes a primacy over other particular loves and excludes specifically marital and parental love; and the special consecration of the body as vehicle of man's presence in and to the world, exercised in work and the use of material goods.

In this brief description, the following elements are considered to be constants in the religious life as it has achieved historical identification down the centuries: *poverty, chastity, obedience* (not here carefully analyzed): *community* (to be distinguished from the purely canonical conception of "common life"); a special *consecration* to God, together with *contemplative union* with him; *apostolic witness and service of some kind.* Ideally, it should now be shown how these elements are related among themselves, how they interact and mutually condition one another. We leave aside an analysis, though it will be partially suggested in our examination of poverty.

Few would deny that poverty has something directly to do with material goods, with having them or not having them, for use and enjoyment and ownership. Today many are inclined to extend the concept to include work, at least work in which the world of matter is involved, and especially in its laborious aspect. There is also an inclination so to broaden the concept of poverty that it stands for a basic attitude touching the whole gamut of life, and especially relations with other human beings. In this broadest sense poverty is the equivalent of availability, of radical detachment. I have no essential objection to this less proper use of the term, provided it is conscious, and provided it does not cloak a desire to escape from the stubborn problems regarding poverty in its more proper sense.

The person who vows religious poverty commits (or rather reconsecrates) himself to use and enjoy material goods in a rational and holy way. But he does more. This something more is what concerns us here. One of its elements is relatively easy to identify. He is entering into a covenant with God and man to share material existence with the members of a particular ecclesial community. This sharing does not necessarily mean that his food, clothing, lodging, medical care or circumstances of burial are exactly the same as those of every other member of the community. It means rather that his *decisions* concerning the use and enjoyment of material goods will be decisions basically shared with the community. This aspect of religious poverty, by which it includes shared decision regarding the use and enjoyment of material goods, points to the partial coincidence of poverty and obedience. This is one good example of the importance of relating the counsels organically, not by mere juxtaposition. The commitment to poverty within religious community includes also a commitment to consult to a special degree the true welfare of the community and of its members.

But sharing material goods, and the decisions regarding them, with a community does not sufficiently specify the gospel counsel of poverty. Who would say (to take an absurd example) that a community totally sharing a material existence possible only for the very rich would be leading a life of the counsels? On the basis of history, one cannot escape the conclusion that material privation in some form belongs to the very core of this form of Christian life. To some degree, fellow religious are called to enrich one another in community not only by sharing the use and enjoyment of material goods, but also by sharing hardship and privation. Though the point cannot be developed here, it seems beyond question that, to be fully of one mind and heart in the spirit of the gospel, fellow religious need to share not only their material goods but their material privation. This remains true even though, apart from the mystery of Christ, material privation tears men apart. Provided the other conditions for genuine gospel community are realized—namely, faith and hope, a real contemplative effort, a genuine living of the other two counsels and compassion for the poor—the sharing of material privation is a most powerful factor in the realization of fraternal charity. A community which is habitually comfortable in material resources is in a weak position to be the salt of the earth and the light of the world.

On the basis, once again, of the historical verification of this counsel, presence to the poor through service of the poor and through some participation in the lot of the poor would appear to be characteristic of religious poverty. I am not here suggesting that physical presence to the literally poor is necessarily a primary motivation in the life of an individual or a community called to follow the gospel counsels. What does seem to be found universally, however, is a special sensitivity toward those who lack the good things of this life, and a tendency, at least, to help them, and to shape the conditions of one's own material existence so that there is congruity between the way the religious lives and the way the poor must live.

It is this note of congruity which provides the answer to the obvious objections that can be raised against any insistence on the experience of material privation and participation in the privations of the poor as necessary for religious poverty. Because poverty is organically joined, within the one human and Christian life, with many other factors, the concrete shape it will take will depend on how the many factors are to come together as an integral life of the counsels. Total identity in food, clothing, lodging, etc. with the most destitute does not represent the ideal of religious poverty. But where the hunger to be of service to the poor, and the desire to share their privation in forms that are appropriate, is no longer found within a religious community, it is hard to see how it can any longer be a community of the gospel counsels.

The result of our analysis so far has yielded this much: religious poverty is a total sharing of goods and privation with a community of the counsels, carrying with it a strong tendency to serve the materially poor and to share appropriately in their condition. The concrete forms in which these two basic elements will be verified will depend on many circumstances: health, culture, nature of apostolic work, etc. A true discernment will recognize the difference between a legitimate (and always somewhat reluctant) accommodation to circumstance, and an acquiescence in a bland middle-class existence. For this discernment to be possible, however, two other facets of the life of the counsels must be brought to bear on poverty. I speak now of consecration and contemplation, and wish to deal with them not as two entities, but rather as two aspects of a deep personal relationship to God and to Jesus Christ.

What gives the counsel of poverty its life and power is the fact that it is the expression, in the life of an individual and community, of a profound surrender to God in Christ. This surrender has its origin in a true conversion, stemming from a revelatory experience of God in Christ. Faith, hope and love are the special terms used to designate what is primary in the response of one who has really encountered Christ. But, because the revelation has been given within the paschal mystery of life, death and resurrection, Christian faith, hope and love, in contrast to a paradisiac verification of these virtues, will be characterized by a certain kenotic or sacrificial quality. To know God in Jesus Christ is to be drawn into the mystery of redemptive suffering; it is to take on a certain affinity with "Jesus who was put to death for our sins and raised to life to justify us" (Rom 4:25).

Historically, some of the men and women who have had such a revelatory experience of Jesus Christ have felt impelled to respond in a distinctive way: irrevocably (hence by perpetual vow), and totally (hence by letting the paschal mystery shape not only their attitudes but the basic form of their lives). In the area of material goods, this means that their hearts have been captured beyond recall by Jesus who "was rich, but became poor for your sake, to make you rich out of his poverty" (2 Cor 8:9). The revelatory moment, the privileged time of beginnings of this relationship with Jesus, is confirmed and reenacted in the lives of religious by the element of prayer and contemplation. Love must remember, or else it will die. The consecration made once for all must be constantly renewed. The element of congruity on which we have placed so much emphasis requires that poverty, to be real and flourishing, needs to feed and to be fed by the contemplative, consecrated relationship of faith, hope and love directed toward God in Christ Jesus.

Have we said anything in this article pertinent to our original question? Are we not far from the original models found in Dorothy Day and Barbara Ward? I think that we have been saying, and perhaps showing, that while no strict demonstration is possible for the thesis that a comfortable middle-class existence is incompatible with the life of gospel poverty, a discerning sense of congruity, attentive to the

historical reality of this form of Christian life, will move always in the direction of a genuine experience of material
privation and sharing the lot of the poor. Professional service
of the poor and of humanity without this dynamism toward
a simple and frugal existence lacks the vigor without which
the life of the counsels is a salt without savor. I have tried
to call attention to the need of considering all the elements
which make up the religious life not in mere juxtaposition,
but as they mutually affect one another within an integral
life of the counsels. It would be a mistake, to be sure, to
impose on all religious a narrow or univocal model for their
material existence. One can also understand that much of the
bourgeois spirit present among some contemporary religious,
especially those moving into more secular life-styles, is a
reaction against certain constricting forms of poverty form-
erly accepted as absolute. Still, at the point at which such a
reaction would bring into the life of religious men and women
a loss of the value and necessity of material privation, something primary would have perished, and religious life would
indeed be imperiled. There is a temptation among religious
today to throw up their hands in despair, and say that we
do not know what poverty means, or that the word has lost
its meaning, or that the reality itself of this counsel as lived
in the past cannot speak to our contemporary world. That
my well be. But before coming to such conclusions, might it
not be well for the individual or community involved first
to remove from the scene the clearly unnecessary forms of
middle-class comfort, and even to take a few bold steps in
experiencing how poor people live? It may then happen that
the grace of God, working within the actual experience of
poverty, might suggest that there are alternative options to
settling down to a comfortable middle-class existence.

8

CELIBACY:
CHALLENGE TO TRIBALISM

As sign of Christianity's transcending of narrow and sacralistic religions in the ancient world, celibacy effectively called men from the idolatry of family, tribe and nation. Today, as our understanding of marriage undergoes profound changes, we need to develop a new understanding of this gift in the Church.

In a scene in Nikos Kazantzakis' *The Last Temptation of Christ*, Jesus is asked by a toothless old woman, who has fed him on his journey, where he is going. "To the desert," he tells her. "Ooo, unlucky devil," she screams at him in rage (her only son had done the same, leaving her without the comfort of grandchildren in her declining years), "don't you know that God is found not in the monasteries but in the homes of men! Wherever you find husband and wife, that's where you find God; wherever children and petty cares and cooking and arguments, that's where God is too. Don't listen to those eunuchs. Sour grapes! Sour grapes! *The God I'm telling you about, the domestic one, not the monastic: that's the true God.* He's the one you should adore. Leave the other to those lazy, sterile idiots in the desert!" (Emphasis added.)

However wild and bizarre the scene (like the book whose theme it epitomizes), it serves to portray part of the scandal and the import of Christian celibacy, and of the Christian gospel, which commends it "for the sake of the kingdom of God." Today as always, Christian celibacy is a word of God, a two-edged sword, of judgment and mercy, of scandal and healing. And it is this precisely with respect to the very center of human life—love, sex, marriage, the family, the tribe, the nation, the race. "The God I'm telling you about" —here, indeed, is the underlying issue. What kind of God is the God of Christians! And what kind of life does this God of Christians invite man to build for himself on this earth? It is in relation to these two questions that Christian celibacy is a word at once disturbing and full of hope.

The issue of celibacy still awaits the kind of solid study that John T. Noonan's *Contraception: A History of Its Treatment by the Catholic Theologians and Canonists* presented for the solution of the contraception issue. The present article, in contrast, is a simple effort, on the basis of a brief historical sketch, to outline one way of conceiving the perennial witness of Christian celibacy.

For clarity, two preliminary remarks are in order. First, Christian celibacy is here understood as the renunciation of marriage by a Christian man or woman, cleric or lay, for the sake of the kingdom of God. Hence this article does not speak formally to the very important status of thousands of Christians who are in the single state as a result of circumstances, not of free option, or into whose decision to remain unmarried the gospel did not consciously enter. Secondly, while much of what will be said here has implications for the celibacy of priests as such, there is no intention of speaking, even tangentially, to that vexed and indeed neuralgic question.

To appreciate fully the meaning of Christian celibacy, we need to see it in its origins, as an ideal emerging in early

Christianity in sharp contrast to the traditions of ancient peoples, including the Jews. This is not to assert that consecrated celibacy is a peculiarly Christian phenomenon, but only to point out the veritable revolution of the gospel, of which celibacy is, in my opinion, an integral part—a revolution that challenges man at the very center of his existence: the family, the tribe, the nation. We need to look at Christian celibacy, and at the Christian gospel to which it is congruous, as a challenge to tribalism. By tribalism I mean here the values of sex, sexuality, family, tribe, nation, and, more broadly, of man as world creator, history maker, at the point where values are absolutized and become the object of idolatry.

Over a century ago, Numa Denis Fustel de Coulanges wrote in French a fascinating study, *The Ancient City,* recently revived in paperback. Its principal theme reveals religion to be the heart of the ancient family, and of those extensions of the family, the *gens,* the tribe, the city. People today often make paganism synonymous with irreligion. Ancient paganism was, in fact, just the opposite—the pervasive presence of the gods in every aspect of human life.

Since the family was sacred, its protection and survival were a religious duty. Not only was celibacy generally unhonored in the world of ancient Greece and Rome, it was at times forbidden by law and usually discountenanced by custom and attitude. A sacred duty of *pietas* enjoined on every son legitimate marriage and child-rearing. So would the fathers survive in their progeny. When, generation after generation, the family gathered in remembrance at the household shrine, the ancestors would be devoutly remembered, and so would live on in their posterity. And as the family grew into the *gens,* the tribe, the tribal city, the same note of sacral domesticity was characteristic. Rome had its gods, and they were not the same gods as were worshiped at Corinth or Athens.

Fustel de Coulanges concludes his study by indicating

the revolutionary change that Christianity brought to this sacralized city. Many theologians and historians today have taken up this same theme of the secularization of the ancient world through the Christian revolution. By preaching a creator God without consort, who transcended nature, who was not to be identified with any one tribe or nation, but was the God of all men and all things, to be worshiped everywhere in spirit and truth, the gospel wrought a thoroughgoing revolution. According to Fustel: "It was not the domestic religion of any family, the national religion of any city or of any race. It belonged neither to a caste nor to a corporation. From its first appearance it called to itself the whole human race."

Even when compared with the beliefs of the Jews in the Old Testament, the gospel of Christ represented a startling challenge. Not that the religion of the Chosen People did not significantly differ from that of their neighbors by affirming a God who was transcendent, free, not tied to the cycles of nature, not the mere projection of instinctual drives. John L. McKenzie, in *The Two-Edged Sword*, has eloquently portrayed the uniqueness of Israel in this regard: "We find in the covenant the center of the unity of Israel: not community of blood nor community of land nor community of language nor a centralized government . . . but the unity of the people of the Lord." Everyone, too, is familiar with the argument for secularization as the product of the Judeo-Christian faith, which Harvey Cox derives from the biblical themes of creation, exodus and covenant.

Nevertheless, Israel's ascent to monotheism, with its corollaries of universalism and divine transcendence, was a long time in the making. Israel continued to maintain that the promises had been made to it, that entry by birth or circumcision into the people carnally descended from Abraham was necessary for all who would share in those promises. It is no surprise, then, to find that Israel's religion was in some sense centered, like that of the other nations, on family, tribe and race. Nor is it surprising to find that, for the Jews of the Old Testament, fruitfulness in marriage was so great a value that both the sterile wife and the virgin who died without marriage and progeny were objects of pity and reproach.

We find in the Old Testament, nevertheless, a few providential foreshadowings of the revolution in values that Christ would bring. On a few occasions where devout and faithful souls clung to Yahweh in faith and trust, even though they had not been given the blessing of offspring, he powerfully intervened to make their marriage fruitful. Such was the case with Sara, wife of Abraham, and Hannah, mother of Samuel.

It is only with the coming of Christ, however, that the break with a religion centered in family, tribe and race is definitively assured. At the very center of the dramatic struggle of Jesus with his adversaries, and of Paul with the Judaizing tendencies in the early Church, was the issue of whether salvation required incorporation into one particular branch of the human family. Both Jesus and Paul make it very clear: birth according to the flesh in *any* human family is unavailing for salvation. A man must be born again, from on high, from the Spirit. A man must be willing to leave father and mother and family, if necessary, for the sake of the kingdom. The barriers (including the religious ones, such as circumcision) between Jew and Gentile have lost their meaning, for Christ in his death and resurrection has called men to a unity that is beyond tribalism. The God of Christians is in this sense definitely not the domestic God. The revolution proclaimed and inaugurated by the celibate Jesus of Nazareth has displaced the center of religious faith from family, clan and nation to the *nova gens Christianorum* —i.e., those who worship God in spirit and truth.

It is only in this context of the transcending of family,

tribe and race through a life that comes to a man as a divine gift, and not from mere human birth, that we can appreciate the call of some disciples of Christ to celibacy. The birth of the Savior himself is a virgin birth, according to the testimony of the Matthean and Lucan infancy narratives. Though the references to the excellence of Christian virginity in the New Testament are few and not without exegetical difficulties, there are enough, I think, to establish the point of view and the pattern that Christian tradition will hasten to take up. Jesus himself speaks of those who "become eunuchs" for the sake of the kingdom, and Paul deals at some length in 1 Cor. 7 with the state of the Christian virgin, who is able, in a way not possible for the married woman, to give undivided attention to the things of the Lord.

Fr. Eduard Schillebeeckx has shown that centuries of development and purification were needed before the authentic Christian motivation for celibacy—the imperious call of the kingdom addressed to Christians who could thereafter "do no other"—was disengaged from motivations of pagan origin such as the yearning for cultic purity. But I am not making a historical point. I am suggesting that when one looks at the Church at its most authentic, he sees in its proclamation of the gospel of universalism, of rebirth in the Spirit and of final resurrection an effective challenge to the tribalism that divides men and dishonors the God who is Creator and Savior of them all. And I am further suggesting that the vocation to consecrated celibacy, as a free renunciation of personal and communal fulfillment through the processes of family, tribe and nation, is, when authentically lived, a congruous expression and reinforcement of this prophetic and revolutionary role of the Christian Church.

Thus far, this article's approach to celibacy may seem to have slighted the harmony between gospel and Church, on the one hand, and the human family, on the other. It may also appear to many readers that its tone has been somewhat triumphalistic. Let me speak now to both these difficulties.

Every word of God, every prophetic instrument of God, is a word that, because addressed to sinful men by the all-holy God, is bitter before it is sweet. This is true pre-eminently of the Word par excellence, Jesus Christ. In the paschal mystery, death comes before resurrection to eternal life; the grain of wheat dies before it can bear fruit; only the lowly are exalted, only the hungry fed. Applied to our present context, this basic paradox of the gospel means that the gospel—and the Church to the degree to which she is faithful to the gospel—blesses and heals the familial, racial and national life of men only on condition and to the extent that gospel and Church effectively challenge the idolatry of family, race and nation, which is the cardinal sin of tribalism. The last word is surely one of salvation, mercy and grace. But as initially received by man, precisely as he is sinful man, the word of the cross is, as Paul said, a word that is a scandal for the Jews and foolishness for the Greeks.

If this is true of the Church as corporate challenge to tribalism, it is true also of the celibate vocation. History testifies to the dramatic threat that celibacy has often constituted to excessive attachments to the ties of flesh and blood. But history—and the personal experience of many celibates today—also testifies to the immense joy and peace that the celibate in the Church can bring to the community of Christian marriage and family. Francis of Assisi is probably the best example of this paradox. The story of his departure from his well-to-do father and family, dramatized in his stripping himself naked of the garments of domesticity, must be set side by side with the incomparable inspiration and peace that the Franciscan spirit through the centuries has brought to Christian family life.

But what of triumphalism? Is the preceding view of the Church and of celibacy simply a consoling refuge and a distortion belied by the facts of ecclesiastical and celibate life? Yes—unless a further sad truth be added, the truth that the Church, and celibates in the Church, when judged by the purity of the gospel itself, have very poorly indeed fulfilled this prophetic role of challenging tribalism and healing the family. And the basic reason is that the Church and its celibates have all too often succumbed to another kind of tribalism, a religious idolatry that apes the very sickness they are called on to heal. The Church can become worldly; the celibates who have directed its course may succumb to an ecclesiastical idolatry, to juridicism, ritualism, power politics, the lordly ways of the Gentiles, to untruth and injustice in defense of untruth, to a protected isolation from the risky and purifying passions and hopes and fears that the rest of mankind has to live with. When this happens, we experience that most monstrous of Christian phenomena: the salt loses its tang, the light is dimmed, the challenge to tribalism succumbs to a worse tribalism, and the healing hand of Christ fails to touch the wounds of marriage, family and the whole ambit of man's life on this earth. Such a condition of the Church and of celibates in the Church deserves the scorn of Kazantzakis' old crone—it is indeed a sterile existence of "eunuchs."

No one who loves the Church can be without anguish when he discerns in it and in its celibates, past and present —and most of all in himself—that blunting of the two-edged sword which occurs when the challenge to tribalism becomes the haven of tribalism. One way of reading Vatican II's effort toward renewal and reform in the Church is to see it as an effort to restore the Church to its pristine vocation to confront idolatrous tribalism in human life. If the celibate vocation is acknowledged to be congruous with this vocation of the entire Church, then it is not difficult to see that a proper understanding of the celibate vocation today is crucial for the Church's reform and renewal.

At the same time, this understanding of celibacy as challenge to tribalism raises the question of whether there can be a future for celibacy in the contemporary world. Suppose tribalism is dead—what then? Is there not growing evidence that the world in which Christianity and Christian celibacy grew and flourished is in its last throes? It may be argued that, at least in the developed countries of the West, the patriarchal family is a thing of the past. The procreative dimension of marriage has yielded primacy to the dimension of marriage as love relationship and love community. This development will doubtless be even more accelerated and universalized as the perfecting of methods of contraception gives the partners in marriage an unprecedented power to say just what their marriage is to be.

One could spell out at great length this revolution that is in process in world and Church regarding the status of woman, man-woman relationships, marriage and family, sexuality, affectivity and personhood. And a great deal would have to be said in answer to the suggestion that celibacy is doomed to decay with the decay of the tribalism that it was called to challenge. To keep this article within reasonable limits, however, I shall confine myself to the following observations:

1. Even in the Western world, tribalism is far from dead. Without appealing to Marshall McLuhan's thesis that we are, on the contrary, witnessing a resurgence of tribalism, one needs only to point to the very special form of tribalism represented by the black and white racism that today threatens the very survival of our nation.

2. But if tribalism still lives, its forms and the forms of marriage and family that it perverts are profoundly changed and changing. If this is so, then the future of the celibate vocation in the Church hinges on its ability to challenge tribalism and support the Christian family in their present reality, not according to the patterns of a dead past. If the celibate vocation can be identified only by comparison and contrast with the vocation to Christian marriage and family, it is essential that those who are called to the celibate life

recognize the *contemporary* reality of marriage and family, conceive their own vocation as complementary to that of Christian marriage, and seek new forms of dialogue and mutual witness and service with their brothers and sisters who are called to the married state.

3. This dialogue can take place only if there is a clear recognition on the part of all that it is the entire Church, and not only its celibate members, that is called to bear witness in the name of the gospel against tribalism, both secular and ecclesiastical, and through that witness to promote both the life of the world, whose center is the family, and the coming of the kingdom. In this great task, all Christians work together as equals, with an equality stemming from their baptism into the Body of Christ. But this basic equality by no means excludes differentiation in the life-styles by which the baptismal vocation finds concrete fulfillment. Equality does not impose uniformity, nor does basic equality require equality in every respect.

I see marriage and family, for example, as constituting the heart of the secular life of man. And I see Christian marriage as the secular sacrament, sanctifying and healing the instinctual, affective and creative forces of men precisely as they are exercised in shaping the world through marriage, family and the derivative institutions that constitute the order of the secular. I see the secular Christian, especially in and through marriage and family, as being the chief protagonist in the secular mission of the Church.

I see the celibate Christian, on the other hand, as called to a special witness against the idolization of marriage and family and derivative secular institutions. If the secular, married Christian stands predominantly (not exclusively) for the Church and for Christ as sanctifier and healer of the secular, the celibate Christian stands predominantly (not exclusively) for the Church and Christ as witnessing against a radical secularization of Christian faith and worship, which is to say, against the sacralization of the world and the domestication of the transcendent mystery of God.

4. Within the life of the Church today, wherever ecclesiastical tribalism continues to blunt the sharp sword of the gospel, there is a special need for celibate Christians, whether priests or laymen, to heed the challenge being addressed to them by the Spirit through the lives and insights of their married brothers and sisters.

5. From the point of view of what has been said here, one can look with both sympathy and critical freedom upon the personalization and domestication of the Church that—overground and underground—is in process in our country today. Liturgies in the home (sometimes rather innovative); floating parishes in which the elements of personal rapport and cultural affinity are characteristic; the tendency to find the Church verified not so much around its traditional structures and institutions and hierarchical authorities as wherever faith and joy and sharing are personally experienced; the desire to let the Church emerge, on a small scale, from the situations and sensibilities of its members rather than on the basis of forms passed on from a previous age or passed down from above—these are only some instances of what I mean here by the domestication of the Church.

Within limits, this domestication is a healthy and necessary thing, one of the remedies being sought for ecclesiastical tribalism, for the excess of objectivization and institutionalization that has deprived the Church of much of the relevance and rootedness she needs for the fulfillment of her mission.

But once this is said—and it is addressed especially to those excessively wedded, as I myself tend to be, to the Church as hierarchical and institutional structure and as set over against the world—something more needs to be said, at least to those who may be oblivious of the dangers of an unqualified domestication of the Church. The community of faith that is the Christian Church is not the ancestral hearth of the Romans, nor the synagogue of an elite race. It may be that the danger of its being captured by the world as verified in the patriarchal family is today, at least in the West, minimal. Far from minimal, however, is the danger of its becoming —in the eyes of many, at least—the Church of a cultural elite.

It has been said that the problem today is not that people are leaving the Church, but that those who are leaving are the wrong people. We should, indeed, be uncomfortable about the fact that the Church is not more of an elite of faith than it is, and with the fact that it is possible, for example, for genuine racism to exist among "good Catholics" and "good priests." But an elite of faith is not always easy to distinguish from an elite of cultural affinity. In the dizzying dialectic of current trends and movements in the Church today, one of the real dangers is that the needed domestication of the Church may turn into a subtle neo-tribalism of a cultural elite. Here is one service that can be rendered by the celibate priests, brothers and sisters who are often part of such movements of domestication. If they are fully conscious of the antitribalistic character of their special vocation in the Church, it will help preserve them, as they struggle nobly against ecclesiastical tribalism, from the irony of creating a tribalistic elitism.

6. But a final word must be said, in an effort to correct an almost necessary imbalance in what has just been said. It is the elite groups, or at least many of them, which are in the forefront of the battle against tribalism being fought on the issues of peace and, especially, of racial justice today. Here we find both married and celibate Christians, side by side, each at considerable risk and sacrifice, challenging the tribal gods of contemporary America. Here, it would seem, we experience no tension, or at least less tension, between antitribalism and domestication. And here, perhaps, in the collaboration of the two central forms of Christian com-

munal existence, the community of Christian marriage and family and the celibate community, we experience the best reminder of what is the vocation not only of some of the Church's members but of the Church as a whole. That vocation is to be the iconoclastic agent and witness of the one true God, who in Christ Jesus has destroyed the tribalistic walls that separate men from their brothers.

9

A LOVE TO BE LIVED

*Purity and passion, characteristic of all Christian love, find
a special verification in the celibate vocation. This throws light
on the likeness and unlikeness between celibate friendship
and the relationship of marriage.*

In recent years many have come to feel that, of the three
vows, it is the vow of celibacy which most touches the heart
of the religious life. For in this vow one decides just how
one is going to expend one's love, which is to say, how
one is going to live. It is not a bad description of what a
religious, or any human being, is called to: a love to be lived.

We are dealing here with a basic need and an inviting opportunity for religious and for the whole Church. The need
is to learn better just how we are to love. The opportunity is
to share with all the men and women of today the love that we
learn daily from Jesus Christ and from his Spirit.

I see three contemporary developments as forming the main
context of what we are reflecting on here. First, the fully adult
status of American religious women is beginning to be recognized, by themselves and by others. As this recognition
grows, it will bring a deeper awareness of their personhood,
their womanhood, their professional and apostolic potential,
and, on the basis of all of these, of their right and responsibilities for an enlarged place in the ministry of the Church.

A second development concerns precisely the ministry of the Church. There is now beginning to emerge a new kind of collaboration between men and women in the Church. Just because the situation of woman has changed profoundly, the style and conditions of this collaboration will be quite different from what they were in the past. A solid and truly contemporary understanding of celibate Christian love as a love to be lived is an urgent need today primarily, I would say, because men and women will be *working* together as men and women for the sake of the kingdom in new conditions and in a new style. It is urgent that we learn to love one another more and better, because without this greater and better love among the men and women of the Church God's people will die of thirst in the desert.

The third development which forms the context of our reflection is the sexual revolution in contemporary America and the world. This is the world to which Christ must somehow speak through celibate love. But before he will be able to speak through religious *to* this world, they must listen to what he is saying *to* them *through* this world—listen and ponder and then respond. What is rock music saying to us about our bodies, about human love and sexuality? What are the beards and the long hair and the blurring of male-female distinctions among the young saying to us? What was the message spelled out in marijuana smoke by more than a quarter million young Americans at Woodstock a few years ago? How do we interpret the current wave of nudity on stage and screen? Premarital and extramarital sex? The divorce court records? And what Marshall McLuhan a quarter century ago called "the mechanical bride"—the employment of sexual imagery by American industry to promote its products—is there something here that we must heed?

It is in this threefold context that we need to share with sensitivity and with great honesty, our thoughts and feelings on celibate love. Celibacy is not only our charism and our mystery—it is our problem. Let me put the problem this way: through an inadequate understanding of the celibate vocation there are enormous human and Christian resources, a powerful potential for love and community, which is not being realized in our lives, and not being placed at the service of Christ, his Church, and our fellow human beings. This inadequacy in our understanding of celibate love, I submit, lies in major part in the fact that we have understood celibate love too much as a prosaic purity, and too little as a powerful passion. The overall resolution of our problem must be a work of integrating the prose and the passion, the purity and the power. This integration is ultimately the work of the Spirit of love, but a better understanding of the element of passion in all human love can open us up to the call of the Spirit.

Let me illustrate with a few quotations. The novelist, E. M. Forster, has one of his characters reflecting on what gift she can bring to the man she is about to marry:

> Mature as he was, she might yet be able to help him to the building of the rainbow bridge that should connect the prose in us with the passion. Without it we are meaningless fragments, half monks, half beasts, unconnected arches that have never joined into a man. With it love is born, and alights on the highest curve, glowing against the grey, sober against the fire. Happy the man who sees from either aspect the glory of those outspread wings. . . . It did not seem so difficult. She need trouble him with no gift of her own. She would only point out the salvation that was latent in his own soul, and in the soul of every man. Only connect! [theme of the entire novel] That was the whole of her sermon. Only connect the prose and the passion, and both will be exalted, and human love will be seen at its height. Live in fragments no longer. Only connect, and the beast and the monk, robbed of the isolation that is life to either, will die.
>
> *Howards End,* pp. 186f.

Apart from a somewhat distorted view of what a monk is, there is a rich insight here. We have all experienced, in ourselves and in others, this living in fragments, this dichotomy between the prose and the passion in our lives. And we are all, I would assume, in search of that rainbow bridge which will help us to connect—only connect.

A similar reflection comes from Louis Lavelle, the French personalist philosopher in his beautiful work, *The Meaning of Holiness* [paperback: *Four Saints*]:

> [The saint] can still be angry and violent, and a prey to passion. He does not seek, as so many do, to disguise those passions. . . . One may say indeed that he mortifies his passions, but they remain a condition and even an element of his holiness. For holiness is itself a passion; or if the phrase offends us, let us call it a sublimated passion. There is in passion a power which holiness needs in order to break away from prejudice and habit. Passion always has its roots in the body; it is passion which stimulates and raises the body to higher levels of living. There is nothing finer than to see the fire which feeds on the most base materials produce at its highest point a flame radiating so great a light.
>
> *Meaning of Holiness*, p. 2

What I am suggesting here has a good deal to do with the theology of concupiscence, and of the gift of integrity. Unfortunately we have come to look upon concupiscence somewhat crudely, as strong or unruly desires, especially in the area of sex. What concupiscence would really seem to be is our inability to *integrate* instinctual drives, spontaneous affection, sensibility, with freedom and rationality. It is a false solution to unruly passions simply to seek to quiet them down or inhibit them. This is an evasion. God gave us instincts, passions, spontaneous drives, to be fulfilled, not to wither on the vine. As St. Augustine pointed out when he contrasted the Stoic ideal of "indifference" with the Christian ideal, Jesus himself and his great apostle Paul were passionate people, sometimes angry, sometimes sad, sometimes tender, sometimes exuberant. Celibacy does call for singleness of purpose, and that phrase, "the single life," is perhaps not a very bad description of this charism. But, if you'll pardon the jingle, to be fully dedicated Christians, the single must tingle. They must be *alive*, fully alive. They are, to be sure, called to accept a certain kind of death: they will never know fatherhood or motherhood in the physical sense, they will not be husband or wife in the literal sense. But they are called to share in the creation of human life at its noblest, namely, life in Christ, life in the Spirit. And this life is possible for all of us only because of passion—the passion of Christ in the sense of suffering, yes—but also in the sense of the intense and integral will to live. Teilhard de Chardin said something which has a special meaning for those who renouce marriage for the sake of the kingdom: "We must have a great love of the world if we are passionately to wish to leave it behind."

One final quotation before I leave this basic aspect of our theme. In one of her short stories, Dorothy Canfield Fisher has an old, old man, who has lived very fully, instructing his great-grandson:

> I tell ye, Joey, I've lived a long time, and I've learned a lot about the way folks is made. The trouble with most of 'em is, they're 'fraid-cats! . . . If ye just about half live, ye just the same as half-die; and if ye spend yer time half-dyin', someday ye turn in and die all over, without rightly meanin' to at all—just a kind o' bad habit ye've got yerself inter . . . Some live, and some die; but folks that live all over die happy, anyhow."
>
> *Hillsboro People*, pp. 48-49

When we religious examine our consciences on how we have lived our vows should we not ask ourselves whether the celibate way has helped us to live and love more intensely, or whether we have bought a certain freedom from sexual disorder only at the price of a diminished affectivity? Should we, of all people, not accept fully the underlying supposition of the hippies, of the young people who often destroy themselves in search of life, the supposition that life is to be an intense experience, that we are to be "turned on." If celibacy does not open us up to being "turned on" by the Spirit, has it fulfilled its purpose?

Somehow, I think, we have forgotten that Jesus himself and his saints throughout history were "turned on" people. Listen to the passionate love that throbs throughout the discourses of the fourth Gospel. Read the tender or indignant words of Paul to the Churches of Corinth and Galatia; the wild letters of Ignatius of Antioch on the road to martyrdom; Augustine's description of the scene at Ostia when he and his mother yearned for eternity; or, later in the *Confessions*, the expresion of his desire for God as a desire to see and hear and smell and taste and touch with the senses of the spirit. I don't have to remind you of the deep and passionate love which so many of the saints manifested not only toward God but toward men—and sometimes toward a particular human beloved. Not long ago I came again upon this reminder that my own "charismatic founder" and his greatest disciple were men of intense personal love: a letter from Francis Xavier to Ignatius Loyola, separated for life by thousands of miles:

> My true Father . . . God our Lord knows what a comfort it was to have news of the health and life of one so dear to me. Among many other holy words and consolations of your letter I read the concluding ones, 'Entirely yours, without power or possibility of ever forgetting you, Ignatio.' I read them with tears, and with tears now write them, remembering the past and the great love

which you always bore toward me and still bear, while at the same time calling to mind the many trials and perils of Japan from which God delivered me through the intercession of your holy prayers . . . In your letter you tell me how greatly you desire to see me before this life closes. God knows the profound impression that those words of great love made on my soul and the many tears they cost me everytime I thought of them."

J. Brodrick, *St. Francis Xavier*, pp. 459f.

Next time you hear a Jesuit retreat master talk about that famous "Ignatian indifference," remember that the words of the "Principle and Foundation" of the *Spiritual Exercises* were written by the man capable of giving and receiving this kind of love.

I have accented so much the element of passion in our Christian love that the reader may be thinking I have forgotten all about the second element, its purity, its singleness of purpose. Obviously this is just as necessary. But purity is not something to be balanced against passion. Rather the two must be integrated. Purity in love is not primarily a matter of restraint, though there are times when it will call for restraint. It is a matter of basic attitude, and I now want to suggest that, in the famous hymn of chapter 2 of Philippians, Paul has given us a beautiful picture of the two basic attitudes a man or woman can take toward human life and human love. He is exhorting the Philippians to live in love and mutual acceptance. He holds up to them the example of Christ Jesus, who, despite his divine status, did not snatch greedily at fulfillment but accepted a lowly condition, even death on a cross. And therefore, Paul says, God has bestowed on him the great gift of becoming *Kyrios*, Lord, proclaimed as such by the whole of creation.

In this passage Paul uses two Greek words which sum up, I think, the choice which confronts every human being. He uses the word *harpagmon:* literally, something to be clung to or snatched at greedily. And in referring to the Father's exaltation of Jesus, he uses the verb *echarisato,* from the same root as *charis* (grace), and meaning, "to bestow as a gift." Let me use two English four-letter words to sum up this contrast. The first is one of the ugliest words in our language— the word *rape.* The other is one of the most beautiful words in our language—the word *gift.* Christ Jesus, says Paul, did not seek happiness, greatness, fulfillment by raping life, by a violent snatching at its beauty. No, he awaited from the Father, in the Father's own good time and way, the *gift* of happiness, greatness, fulfillment. And the Father, pleased because his Son was willing to wait for the gift, bestowed it on him, so that every creature now proclaims, "Jesus is Lord."

We have here, I think, a paradigm for the way we are to love in purity and passion. Passion, the intensity of affection, does not compromise the purity of love. Our love becomes impure only when we snatch at love, greedily, selfishly, only when we are unwilling to wait for the gift to be given. Each man kills the thing he loves, wrote Oscar Wilde. This is true only of the love that is lust. It is not true of the love that is gift, and waiting for the gift. There is no question here of being carried away by love; our love is very imperfect as long as it does not carry us away. What there is question of is the *quality* of the love that carries us away—is it the love that seeks to rape life of its beauty, or is it the love that is willing to wait for the gift? He who saves his life—and his love— loses it; and he who is willing to lose it for the sake of Jesus and his kingdom finds it eternally. Nowhere is this law of the gospel more strikingly true than in the matter of human and Christian love, most of all among those consecrated to celibate love. For if our profession of celibacy means anything at all, it means not that we inhibit the ardor of our love, but rather that our vocation is to bear special witness that love escapes the man or woman who snatches at it, but comes to the one willing to wait for it in patience and hope and freedom.

Once our affectivity takes on this basic quality of openness and reverence before the gift of love, then more particular pastoral directives can find their place in a full and free and healthy life of love and friendship. Let me now touch on some of these aspects. They are familiar, but it will do no harm to recall them.

First, we must grow in love for God and one another by learning to love and cherish our bodies, and particularly those aspects of our bodies which touch on human affectivity and sexuality. A reverent and wondering and joyful and grateful cherishing of our bodies as God's gift to us is part of the Christian spirit. From time to time we should contemplate in wonder and awe these amazing gifts. If our bodies are worthy to be offered to God in celibate love, they are worthy to be loved and cherished by us, in all simplicity and joy. If I have beauty of body, or strength, if it serves as an instrument and sacramental in bringing the healing hand of Christ to other bodies, let me rejoice in this. Let me accept, too, the body that has been given me, and not regret that I did not get someone else's. If, for example, I am a woman and six feet tall—well, even the mountains and hills bless the Lord. If I am a man and my voice is squeaky and my arms and legs puny, let me recall that sometimes it's the little guys who achieve the most. If, when I look in the mirror each morning I tend to get discouraged at what I see, let me remember that Socrates and Abe Lincoln were physically rather ugly people, and that the real beauty, even the real bodily beauty, is the kind that comes from loving purely and passionately, not the kind that comes from birth or from dieting or from the drugstore.

Let us love our bodies, and let us love one another's bodies. If other bodies are attractive to us, thank God for the gift. If they are not, then even here he may be offering a gift if we are alert to discern it. Let us all try to grow in the true beauty of bodily life—in the posture and walk and gesture that express life and hope and compassion and gratitude. With our hands, our lips, our eyes we can do so much for one another, simply, reverently, with love and discretion, and always in search of the love that is gift, not the love that kills the beauty that attracts it.

Secondly, we must accept the responsibility to develop our capacity to love, purely and passionately. This implies many things. It implies that fidelity to vow is a process of becoming. It will take a lifetime to realize the celibate vocation, and it is not adequately realized merely by avoiding thoughts, words or deeds contrary to the sixth and ninth commandments. The celibate life is not primarily a preservation but a search. Developing in celibate love means, moreover, that we respect the rhythms of human growth, both those which are inscribed on the body through physiological and psychic structure and process and those which come from the Spirit. There may be times, for example, when a relative solitude regarding the opposite sex is called for, because the religious, especially in the years when he is experiencing and testing the call of God, is in need of some affective distance. A wholehearted acceptance of being a middle-aged man, or an old woman, and of loving purely and passionately in a way corresponding to these years, is another instance of accepting the rhythm of love's development.

Thirdly, presupposing that an openness to deep and intimate friendship is not only appropriate but even necessary for a healthy celibate love, let me recall some ways in which such friendship can be kept on the right road. The first is that we remember that, before we are anything else to one another, we are brothers and sisters in Christ. It is unfortunate that, when people begin talking about love among celibates, they tend to zero in on intimate friendship in the narrow sense and forget about this prior relationship. Most of us can have relatively few intimate friends; but we should have many, many brothers and sisters. Isn't it a pity that the beautiful term "Sister" has become largely a formal title of address. Let us suppose, for example, a nun and a priest, or a nun and a religious brother, who are drawn to intimate friendship. What inspiration and support should they not find in the fact that their friendship, however intimate it may become in the Lord, is to be built upon the mutual love and reverence which they have for each other as brother and sister in Christ.

A further very important support for deep friendship on the part of religious is the love-relationship which exists, or should exist, between each individual religious and his or her religious community. This squares with what I have just said. I would conceive of a religious community less as a community of friends than as a community of brothers or sisters. A whole talk could be given about this aspect of celibate love. The text for such a talk, perhaps, might be the pregnant sentence of *Perfectae Caritatis* (n. 12): "Above all, everyone should remember—superiors especially—that chastity has stronger safeguards in a community when true fraternal love thrives among its members." The one point I would stress here is the mutuality of responsibility. Let me put both sides as strongly as possible. Sometimes, at least, when an individual is unfaithful to his vow of celibacy, is the primary responsibility before God not with the community for failing to be a community of love and compassion? At the same time, each individual religious, whenever an intimate friendship enters into his life, and especially when it begins to bring basic tensions and even wavering, must remind himself that he has pledged his body in celibate love not only to Christ but to his fellow religious; that they have staked their future on his fidelity to this promise; and that what he does with his body and with his love is not a purely private affair, between himself, his God and his beloved, but also an affair of the beloved community.

A third way of helping to keep our friendships on the right

road is by reminding ourselves that loving as Christ loves
means especially loving the poor. There can be no intimate
friendship without attraction, and the attraction will be in
large part natural. We cannot be friends with everyone. But
when being friends with one or with a few means that I cease
to be a brother or a sister to those around me who are in
special need of my love, there is reason to doubt whether I
am loving my friend in the Spirit. I would, for example, dis-
trust the Christian authenticity of an intimate love in the life
of a religious who was insensitive to the special needs and
suffering of the elderly members of this community. The gift
of love bestowed by God through a dear friend will cease to
be a gift unless it is shared with the poor. A true Christian lover
will sometimes leave the beloved because the poor need him
more. Respect for apostolic mobility is one of the important
signs that a love between apostolic men and women is authentically Christian. At times this means suffering, but the extrav-
agant Father will eventually bless the love in which time and
space do not separate but unite.

A fourth pastoral directive would be to guard, in our language and attitudes, against setting the love of God, passionate
and pure, in opposition to the love of man, passionate and
pure. There is a basic tension here, of course, because we are
sinful creatures, and it would be naive to be scandalized at or
to neglect the tension. But our pastoral principle must be that
there is mutuality between the two aspects of the same love.

Affective prayer, for example, an ardent longing to be in the
presence of Christ, can both free us for warm human friendships and safeguard us within those friendships. But sometimes
the opposite is also true: sometimes the path to affective prayer
and ardent contemplation is opened only when we meet
someone who loves us deeply, who allows us to love them,
who loves us in Christ and into Christ.

A fifth area of pastoral (as well as of more theoretical)
reflection is the question whether and why and how celibate

love is to be differentiated from married love. This is a very large question, but a very important one, and I would like to touch on it briefly, at least. We probably should insist, first of all, on what the two ways of love have in common. The physiologists and the psychologists will have their own point of view on this, I am sure. From a distinctively Christian point of view, there is much similarity. In both forms of human and Christian love, the body, bodily movement and contact, become the vehicle of human and Christian meaning, become gestures and signs of love, the smile, the glance, the touch, the endearing word. Both marital and celibate love must be pure and passionate if they are to be fully Christian.

Still, I feel that there are profound differences between the two loves, almost to the point that we should speak of a qualitative differentiation between them. It is not easy to formulate this difference; it needs, perhaps, to be experienced rather than defined. But we need to try, in both theoretical and more pastoral terms. I don't think we can express the difference primarily in terms of time and space, quantity and number. This has been the tendency in moral theology in the past: the celibate may go so far, and no farther, in a material sense, in the gestures by which love is expressed. I don't mean to suggest a morality or a spirituality of pure intention in this matter of celibate love. There is, quite certainly, the fully unambiguous gesture, marital intercourse, which is a clear sign that a love is no longer celibate. And there are other gestures which, for most people at most times, bring a love-relationship down a road which is no longer celibate. Still, many material gestures of love are ambiguous in character, and human beings, human relationships, and the rhythms of human growth are far too varied to permit of a multiplicity of universal rules about what signs of affection are or are not legitimate.

It seems to me to be rather on the level of quality, and not on the level of quantity or number, that the difference be-

tween celibate and married love is to be discerned. Here are a
few of the ways in which we might possibly formulate the
difference: Marriage, as finding its basic justification in nature
prior to its being sanctified in the Church, is creative in the
Spirit only by first being creative in the flesh. Its immediate
orientation is to marital and parental creativity in the
strictly human order. It is, as Fr. Schillebeeckx says, the
secular sacrament, and its secularity has ontological priority
over its sacramentality. To be complete, to be fully fruitful,
it must be properly and physically genital and procreative.
Celibate love, on the other hand, has an immediate orientation to the Spirit. It takes place on the basis of a free renunciation of the genital and the procreative. It has no secular
justification prior to its validity as sign and instrument of the
kingdom; it is not definable except as a condition of faith and
poverty. It may and must call upon some of the same expressions of love as are employed by marital love, but such gestures now receive a specifically different immediate orientation, namely, to the Spirit and to the kingdom. They will not
so much mediate union in the Spirit as overflow from it. At
the point at which a love-relationship between celibates
would be directed toward the genital and procreative, it
would have lost its meaning as celibate love.

One might also characterize the difference between the two
ways in terms of purity and passion. For the married, the
initial movement of love is one of natural passion, and purity
or singleness enter in derivatively, as part of the process of
drawing that natural passion within the movement of the
Spirit. For celibate love the sequence would seem to be reversed. Passion orientated to the genital and procreative
has been renounced in a vocation to singleness or purity dis-
tinctly stamped with the mark of the Spirit. Passion, of a
non-genital and non-procreative kind, will enter into celibate
love necessarily but derivatively, as an intensification of the

singleness or purity of the man or woman whose life-situation identifies him totally with the kingdom of God which the Spirit is inaugurating on earth.

Finally, there would seem to be distinction between the two modes of love from the viewpoint of universality and particularity. Each of these loves is both particular and universal. But the sequence is different. Marital love opens the partners out to the world in and through the particular beloved. Celibate love, on the other hand, whenever it rests upon a particular beloved, does so only within the broader and prior movement of the gift of self to the community of God's people, which for the religious is concretized in his beloved community.

A final pastoral directive would caution us against isolating celibacy as a love to be lived from the other aspects of an integral life of faith, hope and love. Unless our pure and passionate dedication within the area of the second vow is integrated with a pure and passionate dedication to the poverty of the kingdom and to the obedience of the kingdom, celibate love will not have its fruit. Physical abstinence from sexual activity has no magic power. The comfortable celibate is a contradiction in terms. The rebel celibate and the celibate incapable of personal decision are contradictions in terms. The breakdown of a celibate vocation sometimes takes place through the breakdown of our love for a simple and rugged life, or through our unwillingness to stand the give and take of life within a community with which we have, by the vow of obedience, agreed to share our destiny.

Quite obviously, I have left a great deal unsaid about the pastoral principles which should guide the way in which we live this very mysterious kind of Christian love. It might be appropriate to take our conclusion not from the realm of abstract ideas, but from the person of the one who was both virgin and wife-mother. Mary had a love to be lived, and she lived it perfectly. It was, by the power of God, both a marital and a celibate love. Joseph was her husband, and she loved him as her husband, but with a love totally orientated toward the Spirit. It was a love in which both purity and passion were present and grew together, and the purity preceded the passion, and was its guide. It was not a genital love, but, in the Spirit, it was part of a procreative love whose golden fruit was Jesus, Mary's Son and God's Son. There was perfect purity in Mary's way of loving, and that is why she asked, "How can this be, because I do not know man?" But there was also the perfection of passion in her love, the passion that we see expressed in her exultant song, the *Magnificat*. Mary's pure and passionate love for Joseph, for Jesus, for Elizabeth, for John, for all who entered into her life, was a love which knew how to wait, expectantly. It was a love which was pure gift, and openness to the gift. May God give all of us the great gift of loving in this way, of loving only in this way. For only this kind of love is worthy of the call that has been given us. Only this kind of love can enrich the Church and heal the world.

10

FREEDOM THROUGH DEPENDENCE

The obedience of religious is best seen as a verification of the paradox of freedom through dependence, verified also in other dimensions of human life. Paradigm of this paradox is Jesus himself, totally dependent on the Father, yet fully free for humanity and the world.

"In the beginning God created the heavens and the earth . . . And God said, 'Let there be light. And there was light. And God saw that the light was good' . . . Then God said, 'Let us make man in our image, after our likeness; and let them have dominion over the fish of the sea, and over the birds of the air, and over the cattle, and over all the animals, and over every creeping thing that creeps upon the earth.' So God created man in his own image, in the image of God he created them. Male and female he created them. And God blessed them, 'Be fruitful and multiply and fill the earth and subdue it . . .' And God saw everything that he had made, and behold it was very good." (Genesis 1, passim.)

A Christian theology of creation articulated in the context of a Christian theology of liberation must be grasped in what it is not as well as in what it is. It is not, primarily at least, a scientific or philosophical demonstration concerning the origin of the universe or of man. Nor is it a study of purely natural man, juxtaposed to a study of the supernatural dimension of human existence. Neither is it, strictly speaking, a mere propaedeutic to a theology of liberation. It is rather derivative from a theology of liberation, or at least it has its intelligibility only within the totality of Christian doctrine, Christian experience, Christian mystery, where the primary message, experience and mystery are concerned with our liberation from sin and death through Jesus Christ.

The primary source for a theology of creation, moreover, is the Christian faith-experience, within which it is impossible to separate the experience of creatureliness, dependency, from the experience of freedom, liberation. The biblical authors—Isaiah and the psalmists are examples—counterpoint their praise and powerful deeds in creation: "Thus says God the Lord, who created the heavens and stretched them out, who spread forth the earth and what comes from it, who gives breath to the people upon it and spirit to those who walk in it: 'I am the Lord, I have called you in righteousness, I have taken you by the hand and kept you; I have given you as a covenant to the people, a light to the nations, to open the eyes that are blind, to bring out the prisoners from the dungeon, from the prison those who sit in darkness' " (Is 42:5-7). In the religious experience of the chosen people, liberation is prior to creation. God was encountered in his covenant of mercy with an embattled people before he was encountered as the Lord of all mankind and of the world in general. The movement is from covenant to creation, not from creation to covenant. Moreover, liberation itself finds a central mode of its expression in the language of a new creation: "If anyone is in Christ, he is a new creation; the old has passed away, behold, the new has come. All this is from God, who through Christ reconciled us to himself" (2 Cor 5:17-18).

It is quite legitimate in theological analysis to distinguish a reflection on creation, or "ktisiology," from soteriology, especially in order to signalize a certain dialectic inherent in

Christian mystery. But as theology itself stems from an integral faith and returns to that same faith as its only resolution, so Christian anthropology is an integrity whose "parts" can never be neatly separated out into autonomous units.

The following reflections on man as creature of God will move around the basic symbol of man as image of God, viewed under six aspects: (1) Dependency and Freedom; (2) Soul-Body; (3) Man-World; (4) Man-Woman; (5) Wisdom; (6) Jesus Christ.

My basic thesis—and perhaps it is a hard saying which many cannot hear—is that the mystery of God, and of man with God, contains this basic paradox: freedom lies in the acceptance of creaturehood, of dependency. I will seek to develop this thesis in each of the six parts of my reflection. Man is free to the degree that he commits himself to God in total dependence. The body's dependence on the spirit liberates it for a creativity which it could never achieve in isolation. The material world is liberated for a higher destiny when man governs it. Men and women find their true selves only when they acknowledge their mutual need for one another. Discerning wisdom is needed if we are to distinguish the dependency which enslaves from the dependency which liberates. And: in Jesus Christ, son of the living God, we find the paradigm and the revolutionary force which converts the dependency which is slavery into the dependency which is freedom.

Dependency and freedom

This is the aspect of the Christian doctrine of creation which is most consoling for the believer and most scandalous for the nonbeliever. If man is creature, totally dependent on the omnipotent creator, how can man himself be creative, free? Modern thought from Marx and Proudhon to Sartre has found man's dependence on a provident creator oppressive or inhibiting; human creativity, to be real, must be liberated from the shackles of religion. Theoretical difficulties of this kind gain existential force to the degree that professed believers in man's creatureliness tend to be political and social quietists, so that the Christian pilgrimage comes across to many of our contemporaries as a "trip" to another world induced by hallucinogenic doctrine.

Sometimes theologians will deal with this difficulty in a way which itself represents, in my opinion, a "cop-out," a failure of nerve. Deism and, to a large extent, the scholastic system known as Molinism (from the Jesuit Luis Molina) are inclined to concede that for man really and fully to be man, God must cease to be God, or at least must freely allow man to stake out some ultimate enclave within which God himself is at best a sympathetic spectator, taking his chances in creation on man's not abusing his freedom.

To my mind this line of response is an evasion, philosophically indefensible as well as theologically weak and religiously harmful. Once a theologian or a Christian accepts this implied either-or, the position that God must decrease if man is to increase, we are well on the way toward a God who is not worth serving, a God incapable of fulfilling his own purposes and of sustaining our hope. And we are also far along on the road to misunderstanding man's freedom. Human freedom is not principally in the power to choose A rather than B without inner compulsion or violence from without. This kind of freedom is, to be sure, an important expression of and a condition for man's radical freedom. But the deepest dimension of freedom is that it is man's ability to make himself, in confrontation with the world and also *coram Deo*. Man's freedom does include the terrible power to renounce the covenant fidelity to which God is constantly inviting him. But not even this power of dark creation escapes God's freedom; he knows how to write straight with crooked lines. More positively, when man does, in his better moments, affirm covenant, the very heart of his fidelity is simultaneously God's fidelity to man. Man's freedom is God's gift before it is man's grateful return of gift. "God alone can make something which has value even in his own presence. There lies the mystery of that active creation which is God's alone. Radical dependence upon him increases in direct, and not in inverse, proportion with genuine self-coherence before him" (K. Rahner, *Theological Investigations* I, p. 162.).

Neither Prometheus nor Milquetoast represent the Christian understanding of man as creature, as image of God. Human destiny is not to be liberated from God but by God and unto God. "Man come of age," that Bonhoefferian phrase which has now become shop-worn through insensitive handling, must be filial man, eucharistic man, if he is to be truly man, truly free. Such is the Christian experience of God, doctrinally expressed in the dogma of creation. *Cui servire regnare est—* to be God's servant is to be a king. That beautiful phrase of the Roman liturgy contains, I submit, the heart of this experience. A Christian apologetic can make a strong defense, it seems to me, against the attack on the doctrine of creation as emasculating human creativity, especially if it seeks its model of creation not in *homo faber*, in man the maker of things, but rather in *homo amicus*, in man the subject of relationships, in human love and human community where human beings are self-creative in the process of helping to create the other.

Ultimately, however, the believer defends his faith in God the Creator not with recourse to ideas or models, however excellent, but by a return to his total Christian faith-experience. We are able to believe that we are made in God's image without being reduced to being his shadow because that is the way in which, in our life of faith and prayer, we experience our relationship with him. What is your experience of God in faith and prayer? Do you experience his word as threatening, inhibiting? Is it not rather our common experience that his word is always inviting us to be more than we are, to take initiative, to walk the uncertain pilgrim road, to take a chance with life, to emerge from the many wombs where we would be secure, to grow into our own identity? And, as Christians, do we not find our creatureliness only within a covenant relationship with one who says to us, "I have not called you servants, but *friends*"?

If this experience of God the creator as empowering man for creativity is not given to all in equal measure, we might ask just why it is not. The basic answer perhaps is that God is free to bestow his grace on whom he will and in the measure that he will. But he mediates his grace normally through human agencies. And so, I would suggest that part of the answer lies in the area of our experience of dependency on *authority*, especially parental and religious authority. We can know God under any aspect only on the basis of our experience of one another in the world. An oppressive or smothering exercise of authority by parent, teacher or bishop can create, especially in the crucial area of affectivity, insurmountable blocks to a personal submission of one's life to God's guidance. On the positive side, something of the mystery of the *suaviter et fortiter* is communicated by those persons and communities who, in a love that does what it wills —*ama et fac quod vis*—powerfully evoke and direct our freedom without compelling it. It might be said, then, that a satisfactory response to atheistic humanism rests not so much on adroit apologetics as on the totality of the Christian faith-experience, in which prayer and social relationships, especially with the holders of authority, mediate the mystery of man as image of God, free because of, and not in spite of, his total dependency on his creator.

Soul and body

Man alone, among the creatures of earth, is said to be made according to the image of God. Since it is by his intelligence and freedom that man transcends other creatures, and since God is conceived as pure spirit, the predominant Christian tradition has affirmed that it is in his soul, not in his body, that man is image of God. In recent decades this view has been challenged as dualistic, and exegetes have pointed out that "the Semites know of no dichotomy in man in our terms; the whole man as a complete personality had God's image, manifested especially in the resulting ability to rule over other creatures" (Eugene Maly, *Jerome Biblical Commentary*, p. 11). This insistence on approaching man as a whole person before analyzing and distinguishing is a healthy corrective for a dichotomy, present throughout Christian history but accentuated especially since Descartes, which has had unfortunate consequences, especially in contempt for the body, for matter, for material process. Still we should not forget that without some real distinction of corporal and spiritual principles in man, it is difficult, if not impossible, to sustain the Christian doctrine of life beyond death. By all means let us maintain the unity of the human person, and refuse to consider the body as a mere instrument of the spirit. But the dignity of man in the social, economic and political dimensions of his life can hardly be maintained unless we include in the concept of man as image of God an acknowledgment that, precisely as spirit, he transcends some of the limitations of other creatures of earth. Perhaps what is needed today is a theology which will somehow integrate both an insistence on man's insertion into the world (Marxism, Teilhard de Chardin) and an insistence on man's uniqueness in and over against the world (existentialism).

The ecological question, of which I shall speak in a moment, and the related question of the unity and duality of nature and history, can be dealt with only in the context of the unity and duality of man as image of God. A consideration more immediately pertinent to this program is that the bodily dimension of man as image of God must be conceived concretely, in terms of race, nationality, and culture. The dig-

nity of man as image of God which must concern us is not
the dignity of an abstract man, but of men for whom being
Brazilian, Canadian, Mexican, or being Indian, mestizo or
Wasp is not an accidental determination of image but the only
concrete way in which this particular man can fulfill God's
image in himself.

But the final, and the principal, point that I would like to
make with respect to this soul-body dimension of man as
image of God is that it represents a second verification of the
basic paradox of dependency and freedom. The dependency
of my body on my intelligence and freedom is a dependency
which liberates. When, in the beautiful phenomenon of speech
or song or dance, my lips and tongue and larynx and hands
and feet are made the vehicle of meaning, of communication,
they are brought beyond their limitations to the sphere of
the truly human. *Cui servire regnare est.* Provided of course,
(and what a proviso!) that the spirit reverences the body
which is the vehicle of its self-expression. Here is where the
question of the interrelationship of the various aspects of the
image of God in man first arises. The man who lives out
the paradox of dependency and freedom in his relationship to
his creator will be more likely to reverence his body as he shares
with it the vocation to freedom. In traditional theological terms,
this may be seen as man's return from the alienation of concupiscence to the homeland of integrity. In more modern
terms, we are dealing here with the integration of rationality
and sensibility, reflection and spontaneity. The task of humanistic and Christian education in fostering this integration is
quite obvious.

Man and the world

Through his body man is related to the earth—God's good
earth—and to the universe. This is the aspect of man as
image of God which seems to be predominant in the Genesis

account itself. "Be fruitful, multiply and fill the earth and subdue it." This verse is being read in our day, of course, from the viewpoint of the environmental problem. Only a few years ago it was the vogue in theology to proclaim that Christianity, in contrast with ancient nature religions, had secularized the world, and that this was a good thing. Christian faith was interpreted as being especially congenial to existentialism, and its accent on freedom and historicity. Yahweh was a God who acted powerfully in history, in contrast to the nature deities which entrapped men in cosmic cycles. Today, however, we are being asked to dance to a strikingly different tune, and to accept the charge that Christianity has profaned the world, and that is definitely not a good thing. By its accent on man as master of creation, it is alleged, by its emphasis on history over nature, Christianity has led to a loss of that reverence for the sacredness of nature which was characteristic of pagan religions.

Obviously, there can be no question here of developing, even in outline, a theology of environment. I would agree with those theologians who are now saying that the goodness of the material universe must be cherished, that it cannot be regarded as a mere instrument for man in his pursuit of human destiny, that there is a certain symbiosis of man and his material environment which, especially in the light of evolutionary theory, must be respected, that both scripture and tradition have a broader and richer teaching on man and the world than the bare statement that man is to exercise dominion over the earth. But it is important that this theological response to our ecological crisis not be merely reactionary in character. The call of man to realize God's image in himself through the creative and fraternal guidance of nature cannot be abdicated.

Here again the key would seem to lie in the paradox of dependency and freedom. The earth is ennobled, not enslaved, when man shapes it to his human purposes, provided these purposes themselves be human, and humanly pursued. This third aspect of the image of God as a mystery of freedom through dependency intertwines with the first two. When man, individual and community, finds his true freedom in a total dependency on God, and when he grows in the integration of his own spiritual and bodily forces, liberating the body through a holy subjection to intelligence and freedom, then he will be more likely to avoid both the extreme of a superstitious cowering before the forces of nature, a passive enslavement to cosmic process, and the opposite extreme of an irreverent ravishing of nature in the name of scientific and technological progress. When this happens, then the world itself, already the footprint of God, becomes, in a degree, the image of the image of God. In art, in culture, in civilization, there is a humanization of matter, and in liturgical worship, matter and space and time enter with man, God's image, into the sphere of the divine. *Cui servire regnare est.* To serve the holy purposes of holy men—of a Benedict, of a Francis—is for the good earth, for sun and moon and stars, to share in the human vocation of imaging forth God's beauty.

Man and woman

"God created man in his own image . . . male and female he created them." Some theologians have been inclined to find God's image not precisely in man as an individual, but in man as relational, man in community, and more particularly, in the community of love between man and woman. This is a fourth area where the paradox of freedom through dependency may be studied. It brings us, of course, into another urgent contemporary question, the liberation of woman. There has been rather sharp criticism of the Christian tradition on the part of some recent writers and speakers. Most of us are, I suppose, rather embarrassed by Paul's remarks in 1

Corinthians 11, where man alone is spoken of as the image of God and the reflection of his glory, whereas woman's role is to reflect the glory of man. Paul goes on to say that woman came from man, and not vice versa, and that woman was created for the sake of man, not vice versa. When you add to this biblical teaching the long heritage in inequality for woman in theory and practice in Christian tradition, it is not difficult to see why there should be a "lib" movement today. Here again, however, it is important that our response to this real and important problem should not be merely reactionary. We need, for example, to remember that Paul, in the very same passage, affirms that if woman cannot do without man, man cannot do without woman: there is mutual dependency. And elsewhere (Galatians 3:28) he denies the validity of the man-woman distinction where there is question of dividing what God wants to unite in Christ Jesus.

I would consider that a Christian theology of the man-woman relationship would make much of God's image in mankind as being complete only when there is both man and woman together in love, in community. And I would consider this as the fourth *locus* where the paradox of freedom through dependency is verified. *Cui servire regnare est.* There is, as Paul says, a *mutual* dependency of man on woman, woman on man, and only in the recognition of this mutual dependency can either man or woman or both together be truly free and creative. I would note, once again, how this dependency-freedom is intertwined with the others which I have mentioned, and in both directions. For example, men and women will relate to each other in a liberating and not in an enslaving way when each brings to the covenant of love a harmony of body and spirit, a cherishing of earth and its non-human creatures, and a trustful surrender to God the creator experienced in faith as liberating, and not threatening. And, in the opposite direction, from a deep and liberating relationship of mutual love, men and women can learn to cherish their bodies, to work in harmony with the earth, and to offer themselves with confidence to the designs of a loving God whom they have found in a human beloved.

Wisdom

When God made man according to his own image, he bestowed upon man the capacity to develop that image by growing in wisdom. Especially in those books of the Bible which we call the Wisdom literature, the human vocation is conceived in these terms. I would signalize three aspects of this gift of wisdom as especially pertinent. First, wisdom is a sense of wholeness, a sensitivity to the harmony of the totality of human life, a putting it all together which is not Gnostic or Madison Avenue, which leaves room for mystery and faith and tragedy, but which refuses to acquiesce in a permanently fragmented existence. Are we not in need of wisdom today? Recently some theologians have been saying that contemporary man neither needs nor desires to integrate his life in a unified view, a *Weltanschauung*; the word ideology has become a dirty word in current theology. There is a certain truth in this position: man must walk in faith, without asking to see the distant scene. But this is another thing from saying that man need not struggle to find or to create meaning and wholeness in all that he does and suffers. When man uses his science and technology to get his shirts or his dishes cleaner but only achieves this at the cost of polluting the sources of his life, then we might begin to ask whether he is not in process of destroying himself by refusing the broader perspective of wisdom, which would measure the value of any particular achievement by its contribution to the whole man and to the whole of mankind (cf. Paul VI, *On the Development of Peoples*). Wisdom complements and corrects science by inserting the gains of science into the total organism of human life. Do

we not have here a distinctive challenge to creative and liberated women, and to the feminine present in every person?
Isn't it a predominantly feminine characteristic to refuse the
isolations, the excessive disjunctions, which are the snare of an
exclusively rational mind? Is it not significant that the one
feminine image of God himself in scripture is the image of
divine wisdom, the woman who builds herself a house, prepares her banquet, and invites men to eat the bread of wisdom,
and drink the wine of wisdom? (Prv 9:1-6).

The second characteristic of wisdom pertinent to these
reflections is *discretion*. "I, Wisdom, am mistress of discretion" (Proverbs 8:12). "Does Wisdom not call meanwhile?
Does Discernment not lift up her voice? On the hilltop, on
the road, at the crossways, she takes her stand; beside the
gates of the city, at the approaches to the gates she cries
aloud, 'O man! I am calling to you; my cry goes out to the
sons of men. You ignorant ones! Study discretion; and you
fools, come to your senses!' " (Prv 8:1-5).

It is a discerning wisdom that we need today, a wisdom that,
in the several aspects of man as image of God, is able to *feel*
the difference between the dependency that enslaves and the
dependency that liberates, and the difference between an isolating independence (nondependence) and a freedom that
relates to the Other and to others and thereby frees the person
and the community.

The third aspect of wisdom is specifically Christian, and is
superbly characterized by St. Paul as the wisdom which is
foolishness. "The foolishness of God is wiser than men, and
the weakness of God is stronger than men" (1 Cor 1:25).
This aspect of wisdom pertains undoubtedly more to a theology of liberation than to a theology of creation. Yet creation
itself has its foolishness, the seed that is put into the ground
instead of being eaten. And the prodigality of nature, the
waste! Why so many stars, so many acorns? At least with
the eyes of faith, may we not see here, in this foolishness and

prodigality of nature, a harbinger of the foolishness of the cross? When God speaks his word into the darkness of the dark human creation which is sin, it can only be heard, apart from saving faith, as foolishness. For Jesus Christ, Wisdom Incarnate, there is only one possible role in this crooked world, the role of the crucified clown, the fool. And this brings us to the final aspect of God's image in man.

Jesus Christ

The biblical doctrine of man created according to God's image comes to its peak expression in St. Paul. For him Christ Jesus is, in a unique way, the image of the invisible God (Col 1:15; cf. 2 Cor 4:4). It is in Christ Jesus that we who once were darkness now gaze upon the glory of God radiating in the world: "It is the same God that said, 'Let there be light shining out of darkness,' who has shone in our minds to radiate the light of the knowledge of God's glory, the glory on the face of Christ" (2 Cor 4:6). It is this radiant light of God's glory streaming from the face of Christ which bestows on believers the never fading glory, the restored image of God: "We, with our unveiled faces reflecting like mirrors the brightness of the Lord, all grow brighter and brighter as we are turned into the image that we reflect; this is the work of the Lord who is Spirit" (2 Cor 3:18).

It is when we look at Jesus Christ, the image of the invisible God, that we see embodied the paradox of freedom through dependency which is the key to our understanding of creation and creativity. Jesus Christ is the image of God, he is the Son of God. His whole being is to be son, his whole human existence is filial in character. The word "Father" was ever on his lips, his gaze was constantly toward the Father for the direction of his life. Dependency was the constant law of his life. "I always do the things that please him" (Jn 8:29).

"My food is to do the will of him who sent me" (Jn 4:34). "This commandment (*entole*) I have received from my Father" (Jn 10:18). "Father, into your hands I commend my spirit" (Lk 23:46). In this man as in no other we see a dependency that is total and profound. And yet, was there ever a man who was free as this man was free? "No man takes my life from me. I have power to lay it down, and I have power to take it up again" (Jn 10:18). "All power is given to me in heaven and on earth" (Mt 28:18). "You shall see the Son of Man coming on the clouds of heaven with power and great glory" (Mt 24:30).

In the person of Jesus Christ, then, we Christians find the key to reconciling dependency and freedom. The man most perfectly free is the man most totally filial and eucharistic. From his radical dependency on the Father, the image of God in Christ Jesus reaches out to every dimension of his life. The other aspects of the image on which we have reflected find in him their most flawless embodiment. Spirit and flesh are perfectly integrated in this man whose possession of his body-self is such that he is capable of saying to every man who will ever live: "This is my body; I have given it up for you, and I give it to you to be the life of your body." This man lives in perfect harmony with God's creation, with the lilies of the field and the birds of the air. He commands the wind and the waves and they obey him. He rules the earth without oppressing it; his yoke is sweet, his burden is light. This perfectly filial man is therefore perfectly fraternal, and he gives his body in intimacy not to one particular woman who bears the children of his flesh but to that one Woman for whom he delivered himself up, on whom he has breathed forth his Spirit, that he might present her to himself as a spotless bride, that Woman whom he calls to liberation: "The Jerusalem above is free, and she is our mother" (Gal 4:26). Finally, this filial, eucharistic man verifies perfectly in human flesh the wisdom of God. Like Wisdom of old, he stands in the temple and cries out, "If any man is thirsty, let him come to me and drink" (Jn 7:37). His side is pierced on the cross, and the living water of the Spirit flows forth to be the wisdom of the Church, the wisdom of a people which, in a crooked world, is constantly called to share and celebrate God's wisdom in that never ending feast of fools which is the life of Christian faith.

At the end of this reflection on the mystery of freedom through dependency as we see it verified in the different aspects of God's image in man, I have the feeling that it not only needs to be complemented by a theology of liberation, but that it may appear to belong to a totally different world than that in which theologians have been speaking of liberation and human hope. Be that as it may, I conclude with some simple convictions, born of these reflections, on a few of the needs of those who are struggling today, on many fronts, to restore the disfigured image of God to man and his world.

We have need, first of all, of *contemplation*. Without the bread of wisdom and the wine of wisdom our humanity dies of starvation and boredom. Without wisdom's sense of what is congruous, wisdom's feeling for wholeness in our humanity, we become fragmented men. The world today needs contemplative men and women. That most men and women will have to find contemplation in the midst of a very active life only increases its importance. When believers do not pray, the people perish.

Secondly, we need *eucharist*. I include in this statement the celebration of the Eucharist, celebrations worthy of free men, in which we give expression to what we really want to say. But I mean much more by eucharist *thanksgiving*, gratitude for life, consent to being, the will to be alive in this world. Unless we are able to celebrate God's gifts to us in creation and in the new creation, then our struggle with the principalities and powers will be grim and joyless. The world today needs eucharistic men and women.

Finally, we need the spirit of *reconciliation*. I am speaking here not so much of the reconciliation of alienated groups, and I acknowledge that the spirit of reconciliation is quite compatible with the acceptance of the need for creative conflict, even among brothers. But I am thinking more broadly of what the scholastics called *concordantia oppositorum*, the ability to let ideas and values which are in tension with one another be what they are, without reduction, the patience to live with paradox. For the theme of this conference, this means that dependency and freedom, being created by another and being creative oneself, do not necessarily annihilate each other. We may legitimately discuss what kind of dependency we are willing to accept and what kind of freedom we are seeking. But in Christ Jesus, God's perfect image, we who believe in him will discover that it is the man who is filial and eucharistic who possesses himself and his world in freedom. "Happy the gentle: they shall have the earth for their heritage" (Mt 5:5).

11

CAN MAN ENCOUNTER GOD TODAY?

Is it possible to reconcile the viewpoints of secularity and sacramentality in the sphere of religious experience? Yes, it is, provided we accept a negative theology and a "dark night" spirituality, and provided we add to the traditional contemplative adage, pati divina, *a contemporary* pati humana.

A widely circulated Charlie Brown poster may serve appropriately as text of the following reflections on prayer: "No problem is so big or so complicated that it can't be run away from." Who can say anything really new about prayer? And who can speak about prayer except out of his own failure to pray as he ought? We cannot speak about prayer as we would talk about the structure of the molecule or the eating habits of the fruit fly. It is something which is part of ourselves as persons, something which we *are* as Christian persons, something which we all do, rather badly, and which we want to do better. The better part of these reflections will be the beginning, where I will simply present brilliant and provocative thoughts by some eminent writers. I will not be deducing anything from these quotations, or even commenting on them. I do not offer them as representing, necessarily, my own view. But all of them have something to do with what I shall be trying to say. The authors are identified at the end of this chapter.

1. In our era, the road to holiness necessarily passes through the world of action.

2. For him who has not suffered, the brother does not exist.

3. Two and two only absolute and luminously self-evident beings, myself and my creator.

4. Lo, I have prayed to God. *Reason*: Now, what do you want to know? A. All these things which I prayed for. R. Sum them up briefly. A. I desire to know God and the soul. R. Nothing more? A. Absolutely nothing.

5. And what is this God? I asked the earth and it answered: "I am not he," and all things that are in the earth made the same confession . . . I said to all the things that throng about the gateways of the senses: "Tell me of my God, since you are not he; tell me something of him." And they cried out in a great voice: "He made us." My question was my gazing upon them, and their answer was their beauty . . . I asked the whole frame of the universe about my God, and it answered me: "I am not he, but he made me."

6. We must face up to the fact that the call of Christ *does* set up a barrier between man and his natural life . . . By calling us he has cut us off from all immediacy with the things of this world. He wants to be the center, through him alone all things shall come to pass . . . *He is the Mediator,* not only between God and man, but between man and man, between man and reality . . . Wherever a group, be it large or small, prevents us from standing alone before Christ, wherever a group raises a claim of immediacy it must be hated for the sake of Christ . . . For the Christian the only God-given realities are those he receives from Christ . . . The path . . . to the God-given reality of my fellow man or woman with whom I have to live leads through Christ, or it is a blind alley . . . Christ stands between us, and we can only get in touch with our neighbors through him. That is why intercession is the most promising way to reach our neighbors, and corporate prayer, offered in the name of Christ, the purest form of

fellowship . . . Though we all have to enter upon discipleship alone, we do not remain alone. If we take him at his word and dare to become individuals, our reward is the fellowship of the Church.

7. When we come before God with hearts full of contempt and unreconciled with our neighbors, we are both individually and as a congregation worshiping an idol . . . There is therefore only one way of following Jesus and of worshiping God, and that is to be reconciled with our brethren.

8. I should like to speak of God not on the borders of life but at its center, not in weakness but in strength, not, therefore, in man's suffering and death but in his life and prosperity . . . God is the "beyond" in the midst of our life.

9. God is teaching us that we must live as men who can get along very well without him. The God who is with us is the God who forsakes us. The God who makes us live in the world without using him as a working hypothesis is the God before whom we are all standing. Before God and with him we live without God. God allows himself to be edged out of the world and on to the cross.

10. Now that it has come of age, the world is more godless, and perhaps it is for that very reason nearer to God than ever before.

11. There is always a danger of intense love destroying what I might call the "polyphony" of life. What I mean is that God requires that we should love him eternally with our whole hearts, yet not so as to compromise or diminish our earthly affection, but as a *cantus firmus* to which the other melodies of life provide the counterpoint. Earthly affection is one of those contrapuntal themes, a theme which enjoys an autonomy of its own . . . When the ground bass is firm and clear, there is nothing to stop the counterpoint from being developed to the utmost of its limits.

12. By means of all created things, without exception, the divine assails us, penetrates us and moulds us. We imagined

it as distant and inaccessible, whereas in fact we live steeped in its burning layers. *In eo vivimus.* As Jacob said, awakening from his dream, the world, this palpable world, which we were wont to treat with the boredom and disrespect with which we habitually regard places with no sacred association for us, is in truth a holy place, and we did not know it. *Venite, adoremus.*

With these texts, and the various resonances they may evoke, I would like now to circle around the question posed in the title of this essay: Can Man Encounter God Today? Let me begin by suggesting that, at least in Roman Catholic circles, the crisis of prayer and faith has come about, in large measure, from the meeting and clash of two very different viewpoints: the theology and spirituality of sacramentality (conceived as encounter with God and Christ), and the theology and spirituality of secularity. More than a decade ago, due to the influence of ecumenism, personalistic philosophy and other currents of thought, Catholic theology bade an unfond farewell to the post-Tridentine accent on *ex opere operato,* judged to be dangerously open to mechanistic or magical interpretations, and began to speak of our encounter with Christ in the sacraments and in the whole life of the Church. Edward Schillebeeckx's little masterpiece, *Christ the Sacrament of the Encounter with God* (New York, 1963), was undoubtedly the principal agent, at least in this country, of disseminating this thrilling new and personalistic expression of Christian sacramentalism. The influence of Teilhard extended the range of this encounter with the divine to the whole of the evolving cosmos, conceived as the diaphanous, epiphanic milieu which throbbed with the presence of God. Vatican II reflected very strongly this reawakened sense of the divine presence throughout the whole of human and cosmic life.

But hardly had we finished proclaiming the joyful message that God and his Christ were to be encountered everywhere when we became aware of other voices, announcing that the

God whose presence we were celebrating was really an absent God; that the God to whose revealing sacramental word we were responding in joyous faith was really a silent God, a God who does not speak to man; and in fact, that the living God who called us to life had really died, as Nietzsche had proclaimed. Even though many versions of the absence, silence or death of God were not properly atheistic, the very least that this current of secular Christianity would settle for was that he was a God who was totally Other, not to be encountered. His very otherness was, for some like Friedrich Gogarten, a liberation of man to do his rational thing in the world unhindered by intrusion from inhibiting or distracting deities, as in ancient paganism. But in any case it was futile, if not blasphemous, for man to look to God as a dialogue partner within the finiteness of daily human existence.

The implications of such a challenge to a spirituality of encounter were plain. And the doubts regarding prayer that began to afflict many Roman Catholics, particularly priests and religious, were not merely whether the God-encounter in interpersonal relations and social action was now sufficient without the God-encounter of formal prayer, but whether God was to be encountered at all, whether Christ was to be encountered at all. On this last point many felt, quite wrongly or at least quite oversimply, that critical study of the Gospels had taken away the Jesus of history; and as for the glorious Christ—well, encounter with him seemed as much an impossibility as encounter with God.

It was not merely the theology of secularity which disturbed the spirituality of encounter; the picture is more complex. The scientific world view, with its progressive and inexorable erosion of the divine beachhead in the world of nature and of man, was an important factor. But it is unlikely that this triumph of the scientific world view alone would have so shaken the foundations. Among many influences, the ever more patent inability of the Church and her theologians to meet the new problems raised regarding accepted dogmas of faith and regarding an immutable natural law tended to bring disturbing doubts where previously there had been only assurance of divine guidance through the Church. And the "last hurrah" (still echoing) of a centralized, uncollegial and rather fearful bureaucracy has not helped; neither have some of the excessively shrill denunciations of it. But, most of all, the terrible evils of the last fifty years—Dachau and Vietnam and American cities in flames—have left most of us silent or stammering in the face of the obvious questions: Where is your God? Where is the Christ you claim to encounter?

This, it seems to me, is where we are now: not merely addressing in a new context the perennial problem of contemplation and action, but asking ourselves whether the theology and spirituality of God-encounter and Christ-encounter are really viable, or whether they must yield to a theology and spirituality in which man is alone in his work in the world, at least so far as any experience of God is concerned. Can man today really encounter God, either in formal prayer or in standing with his neighbor?

My very small contribution to an answer to this question is to suggest, first, that a more adequate answer will be a strongly qualified Yes; that the qualification is to be made with help from the theological and mystical traditions; and that more distinctively contemporary expressions must be found for these traditional expressions of Christian faith.

My impression is that the theology and spirituality of the encounter with God and Christ have suffered from expecting both too much and too little: too much in the sense of not taking with full seriousness that this is an encounter in the darkness as well as in the light of faith; too little because the God and the Christ who tended to emerge as dialogue partners in the encounter were a diminished God and a diminished Christ, not the *Deus semper maior* nor the Christ whose riches are unfathomable. And if encounter spirituality is to sustain the meeting with secular Christianity, it is in need of speedy help from two interrelated streams of Christian tradition: the theological tradition of the negative theology and the spiritual tradition of the dark night.

Let me seek only to identify rather than to analyze this two-fold tradition. The negative theology formulates the biblical teaching and the Christian experience of the mysteriousness and transcendence of God in such terms, familiar to many of you, as: We know of God rather what he is not than what he is; we know that God is, but not what he is or how he is, etc.

Frequently the austerity of this negative theology is domesticated by appeal to the Incarnation, to the fact that, incredibly, the God who is totally Other has spoken to man in Christ, in whom the Father's image is manifest to us. This is undoubtedly true, if properly understood. But this manifesting Word which is Christ is itself unfathomable, and to the negative theology we must add a negative Christology, so that we may say in truth: we know of Christ rather what he is not than what he is. The disciple of Christ has not less but more appreciation than anyone else that the God of our Lord Jesus Christ and Jesus Christ himself in glory are not to be encountered in the way in which we encounter other human beings.

We may perhaps even go a step further, and to the negative theology and negative Christology add a negative anthropology. Are we so sure that we really do encounter the neighbor? Joseph Pieper has brought out in his little work, *The Silence of St. Thomas,* that the creature as creature is mystery to us, and somewhere, I think, St. Augustine has said that it is only in eternity that we will really see the neighbor, when we see him in God.

The mystical corollary of this negative theology is the spirituality of the dark night. As I understand its expression in *The Ascent of Mount Carmel,* it maintains that the encounter with God is really a journey toward encounter, a journey characterized by a certain darkness, and one which entails the progressive surrender of assuring images, concepts, feelings, which we must leave behind not because they are evil but because they are not God. "We are not he," the creatures call back to our inquiry; at the point at which we would stop the journey, the creature becomes an idol, the value becomes a disvalue, and we are no longer walking by faith.

But if this negative theology and this spiritual tradition of the dark night can help to purify, and thereby to preserve, whatever is valid in the theology and spirituality of encounter, they will not succeed in doing so unless they find formulations more congenial to contemporary Christian experience than we find in St. Thomas, St. Augustine or St. John of the Cross. The formulations must, of course, emerge from the experience of some Christians that they may in turn guide the further experience of all Christians. I do not know what the formulations might be, but I now propose, still circling around this theme, to suggest some of the ingredients, at least, of the experience itself.

The first ingredient is aptly expressed in a statement of the French Dominican, Dominique Dubarle, "Modern humanity . . . [is] going through nothing else but a . . . democratization . . . of that night of the spirit mentioned by [St. John of the Cross]." [1] What Pere Dubarle is suggesting, I think, is that we are to look for the verification of the dark night not merely to the formal contemplation of the privileged few, but to the integral Christian experience of the entire people of God. In this period of cultural breakdown and transition, it is not only prayer forms which must be relinquished at God's call; it is a whole complexus of now unviable expressions of the Christian faith: institutional, liturgical, devotional, existential. Nor is it a question merely of substituting one set of such expressions for another. The evolutionary dimension of human

[1] Quoted by C. Geffré in "Desacralization and the Spiritual Life," in *Concilium*, 19, p. 112.

life, the mobility, relativity and atomized character of man's life today, means that we have to accept living with fewer forms, especially fixed ones, in our journey toward God. This means walking for the most part in the dark, not quite sure just where we are going—it means the democratization of the dark night.

And so a good part of that asceticism of faith which is both a necessary condition for progress in prayer and the fruit of such progress will consist, for us today, in a simple willingness to live in a world and in a Church which are undergoing a cultural and institutional breaking down. One of the great enemies of true prayer is anxiety, basic anxiety, I mean—that unwillingness to let things be as they are, that "they can't do this to me" attitude. I am not suggesting here quietism or stoicism in the face of evils in Church or world, or a blunting of sensibility as the many human things we have come to love are torn from us. Rather I am speaking of a certain buoyancy, a persevering zest for life, a willingness to let things be as they are (at least as the given, as the starting point), a certain patience and withstanding of pressures (akin to the Pauline *hypomone*), especially the pressures of ever threatening despair, as we both press forward to the goal and wait for the Lord:

Young men may grow tired and weary, youth may stumble,
   but those who wait for the Lord renew their strength,
They put out wings like eagles
They run and do not grow weary
Walk and never tire

(Is 40:30f)

A second element in that journey of faith in the dark night where a qualified encounter with God and Christ takes place concerns the *tone* of our sacramentality. It will be, I think, a sacramentality that is more person-centered and less nature- or cosmos-centered. Liturgically it will be clearer that the sacramental sign is not the water or the oil or the wafer but the human gesture, the address of one person to another: I baptize you; I forgive you in the name of the Father, Son and Spirit; I take you for better or for worse, etc. Extra-liturgically, we will have to accept that the fraternity with nature in the cosmic sense of a Francis of Assisi can no longer be ours. Though communion with nature in its relatively untouched (and unblemished) state will probably always have a place in our lives, this will be only a kind of counterpoint to the more basic finding of God as we may within the human city, where God manifests himself in a world worked on by human creativity of a distinctively urban style.

A third ingredient of a contemporary Christian experience which is a faith-encounter with God I would like to sum up in the phrase: *pati humana*—to be receptive to, and to be vulnerable by, fearless exposure to human life in its integrity. One of the traditional terms used to describe the purifying mystical experience is *pati divina*: to be receptive to, and vulnerable by, the searing and purifying presence of the living God. Today, it seems to me, there is need to give prominence to what was always implicit in Christian spirituality, namely that the journey of faith in the dark night is not only a plunge into the mystery of God but a descent into our humanity, a willingness to be human among humans. It is here, I think, that we modern Christians are being called to give a distinctively new expression to the imitation of Christ, to discipleship.

I would see a double aspect of this stance of *pati humana* as characteristic of Jesus and of his disciples. The first aspect is expressed by the beautiful statement of Paul: "The Son of God, the Christ Jesus that we proclaimed among you . . . was never Yes and No: with him it was always Yes, and however many the promises God made, the Yes to them all is in him. That is why it is 'through him' that we answer Amen to the praise of God" (2 Cor 1:19-20). Jesus as the man of unswerving affirmation, the perfectly responsive person, the man who always went to meet life, who always said Yes to life, most profoundly to that life which came to him from the Father—"I do always the things that please him"—but also to whatever came his way from his sinful fellow men. "I have compassion on the crowd." To be willing to let both God and man shape our destiny—*pati divina* and *pati humana*—this is the Yes, always Yes, to which we are called.

The second aspect of this *pati humana* is what Jesus did, and what we must do, when life does not respond to our Yes with a Yes. The author of Hebrews tells us how Jesus stood under the No—the surd of untruth and ungoodness—present in human life. He "endured a cross, despising the shame." Endurance—*hypomone*—standing up to adversity by what we may best call vulnerability, an availability for the other—for the Father and for men—that perseveres in the midst of adversity.

I will return in a moment to a more practical description of how this *pati humana* can enter into our Christian experience of praying always or finding God in all things. But first I must mention the last ingredient of a truly contemporary Christian experience, and perhaps it is the most crucial of all, and the most difficult. Its most radical expression is the saying of Jesus on which one of the statements I quoted from Bonhoeffer was based: "If you bring your gift to the altar, and there remember that your brother has something against you, go first and be reconciled to your brother—then (only then) come and offer your gift" (Mt 5:23-24). Our most basic problem in persevering in prayer today is not that there are "death of God" philosophers or theologians, or that science has called in question whether God intervenes in human life or that we are in a period of profound cultural transition. No—it is because our brother has something against us, because outside of prayer, outside of liturgy, we are unreconciled and not fully converted to Christ. Our brother, our sister, is crying out against us, from the ghetto, from the hamlets devastated by war, but also, less dramatically, perhaps, but no less really, from the infirmary of our convent or religious house, from the desks where our young students sit, from the other end of the dining room table in our suburban home. I realize that one can oversimplify. I realize that prayer makes such reconciliation of brothers possible, as well as being made possible by reconciliation. I appreciate that life in the ghetto, or direct participation in the peace movement, is not for all, and that there are many undramatic and humble ways of engaging in the unending task of reconciliation. Still, as an accent, as an opening out to the call for continual conversion, we have to allow ourselves to realize over and over again that our brothers and sisters have something against us.

The last thing I would like to do in pursuing this theme of the possibility of an encounter with God in the conditions of contemporary life is to describe what I feel is the ideal to which we are tending as men and women of prayer in the world of today. The traditional expression of this ideal is finding God in all things, praying always, habitual prayer, contemplation in action, etc. I would describe it as a *response* to value in each human situation, and I would set it in contrast to merely *reacting* to situations from instinct, prejudice or habits which represent nature and not person. The man or woman of prayer will be the one who, habitually, in the little, the big and the middle-sized moments of life, will be able to say Yes, the particular Yes which the situation may demand, while resisting and even transforming the particular No which that same situation contains; the one who remains in the vulnerability of faith and hope, who will not seek to crawl back into the security of the womb or employ any of the myriad of artifices and evasions of which we are all such past masters; the one whose response to the situation will not proceed from mere instinct of nature, but from personal freedom, a response given *from* the Spirit, the inner dialogue-partner, and from the charity which he pours forth in our hearts, and a response which is addressed *to* the Spirit, present in the situation itself, and especially in other human beings. Traditional theology speaks of what I am talking about in terms of the progressive return of Christian man to the state of integrity, his progressive liberation from concupiscence, from the flesh in the Pauline sense, from selfishness.[2]

Much more could be said by way of general description, but let me now particularize and illustrate. Can we be men and women of prayer in the *little* moments of life? There are a million and one little situations in life, and it is the man or woman of prayer, the responder, the Yes-sayer, the vulnerable one, who is able to assimilate and share the riches that every moment of human life contains. Watching television, for example: making the most of the commercials, whether it be the girl in the bikini, the plea to help the tiger keep his job, the tasteless shaving cream ad, and so on. Or take the experience of driving, not only the exhilaration of the superhighway but the stop and go experience of the Long Island Expressway. Or the missed connection. The broken tooth. That morning "blah" feeling. The lost ticket. The burp that escapes you at that important cocktail party. The sticky and smelly summer subway ride. The broken shoelace. But take not only the hard things, the discouraging things. Take the sudden exposure to the beauty of a person, from seven to seventy; the unexpected and undeserved expression of esteem or love; the gentleness of the strong; the silent sympathy of strangers when you are embarrassed; the gift of an ordinary sunset.

There are also the larger situations: the moment you finally come to terms with the fact that you are married to an alcoholic; the phone call from your neighbor reporting that there is a black family "trying to bust our block"; the day you realize that you are forty or fifty or sixty; the day you are

2 Cf. Karl Rahner, *Theological Investigations,* I (Baltimore, 1959), pp. 347-382.

told you have cancer; the day you realize that you are finished as a teacher, or a surgeon, or a pastor. Or the day when the secondary supports of your priestly or religious or marital vocation suddenly collapse, and you ask yourself if there are not really other options open to you. The morning the encyclical on birth control came out, or the day you were asked to sign a protest against it.

In all such situations, small, large or middle-sized, we either respond or react, though most frequently there is something of both. But to the degree that we are men and women of prayer, the element of true response, of letting the Spirit speak through us to the situation and through the situation to us, will be predominant. And progress in prayer means reacting less and responding more, and enjoying it more.

Those of you who are familiar with the work and philosophy of Monsignor Robert Fox in Harlem will recall his phrase of "chewing up" reality, how he speaks of "not pulling down the shades on 'the Street'." This constant moving toward reality, accepting it for better or for worse, being vulnerable to it—this is what it means to pray always, to find God in all things, to be a contemplative in action. It has its difficulties, of course. It is a goal never really achieved. But it is the great adventure of life.

I suspect that we are all in agreement that this is what we are aiming at for ourselves, and especially for our young people today, even though each one would state this ideal in a different way, with different accents. So our problem of understanding prayer may not be a problem of knowing what it is, but a problem of being able to describe and relate the conditions which make it possible, for this individual or this group, in a given situation of human and Christian life, and within the limitations, opportunities and atmosphere characteristic of today's world. Among the many conditions of genuine prayer at all times, we should not forget the importance of *conversion*. I mean not only that continuing conversion (which is not so much an event as a permanent posture, more or less the vulnerability I have spoken of), but conversion as an event, no more than once or twice in a whole lifetime. I mean those rare and privileged moments when God gives us the grace to realize that we cannot live without him, and that we achieve our humanness to the degree that we live with him, and with one another in him.

The authors quoted on pp. 142-144 are:

1. Dag Hammarskjold, *Markings* (New York, 1965), p. 122. To which a *New York Times* reviewer responded, sagely, that it was also true that today the road to action necessarily passes through the world of holiness.

2. Soren Kierkegaard.

3. John Henry Newmann, *Apologia Pro Vita Sua* (London, 1888), p. 4. The original version had "supreme" in place of "absolute."

4. St. Augustine, *Soliloquies,* Book 1, Ch. 2, in *Fathers of the Church* I (New York, 1948), p. 350.

5. St. Augustine, *Confessions,* Book 10, Ch. 6, trans. F. Sheed (New York, 1943), p. 216.

6, 7. Dietrich Bonhoeffer, *The Cost of Discipleship* (New York, 1963), pp. 106-113 *passim,* pp. 144f.

8, 9, 10, 11. Dietrich Bonhoeffer, *Letters and Papers from Prison* (New York, 1962), pp. 165, 219, 175.

12. Teilhard de Chardin, *The Divine Milieu* (New York, 1960), p. 89.

12

THE IGNATIAN EXERCISES: CONTEMPLATION AND DISCERNMENT

Like Ignatius himself, his Exercises *are a remarkable blend of contemplative and decisional prayer, which correspond to a basic human duality of doing and being, purpose and meaning, acting and receiving.*

What I would like to do in this essay is to examine the *Spiritual Exercises* of St. Ignatius Loyola from a particular point of view. My aim is not to persuade anyone to read this little book. Nor am I interested at the moment in persuading anyone to make an Ignatian retreat. For one thing the book is somewhat unreadable, and secondly, it was not written in order to be read, except in a very special context. I would, if anything, counsel most people against reading it as they would read an ordinary spiritual classic. My primary aim is rather to suggest that what Ignatius did in his own Christian experience and what he expressed in his *Spiritual Exercises* is something which all of us are called to do as Christians, men and women of prayer: to integrate the prayer of discernment or what I would call decisional prayer and the prayer of contemplation. And I will be further suggesting that prayer, if it is to be integral, must be both decisional and contemplative because this is the way *life* is as long as we are on pilgrimage. Finally, I will say a word about what all this has to do with the present crises of our society.

Before I say anything about Ignatius' *Exercises*, let me say a little about Ignatius himself—about Iñigo de Loyola, as he was called, before he decided to take the name Ignatius of Antioch, the great bishop and martyr of the second century. The author of the *Spiritual Exercises* was a Spaniard, more precisely a Basque. Like Francis of Assisi he was small in stature. He is generally presented as rather stern, sober, rational—and undoubtedly he was. But his biographers also tell us that, being a Basque, he grew up knowing how to sing and dance; that once in Paris, he sang and danced, despite his limp, to cheer up someone he was directing; and that in his later years in Rome, when he was constantly plagued with pain and sickness, he got more relief when someone sang to him or played the guitar than when he took the doctor's medicine.

He was a man who knew how to wait. He had an incredible capacity for waiting (and this is one of the keys to his understanding of the discernment of spirits). His conversion took place in 1521, when he was 30 years of age. He did not take vows as a religious till 1534 (age 43); he was ordained in 1537 (age 46) and waited a year and a half before celebrating his first Mass at Christmas in 1538, in the chapel of the Crib at St. Mary Major, in Rome. The Society of Jesus was not founded until 1540, almost twenty years after his conversion; the Constitutions did not get approved until 1552, and he died in 1556, at the age of 65. He died alone, this man who had written in the primitive Constitutions of his Society, "The manner of life is ordinary." The man who wrote the *Spiritual Exercises* was not a priest, and that is something we should remember today as we try to appreciate the priestly and prophetic role of every baptized Christian.

The *Spiritual Exercises* are really a distinctive kind of art form, a crystallization and socialization of the Christian experience of this remarkable disciple of Christ. I will be speaking of a certain duality of discernment and contemplation in the *Exercises;* so let me speak first of this same duality in the Christian experience of Ignatius himself. Ignatius of Loyola was a mystic, a Trinitarian mystic. The researches of the last three or four decades have brought this out. From shortly after his conversion until his death, he received extraordinary gifts in prayer, intellectual visions of the Trinity, for example. He himself writes of himself: "On one occasion, he was given an intellectual understanding accompanied with great spiritual joy, of how God created the world." Or again: "On many occasions, and for a long time, during his prayer, he saw with his interior eyes the humanity of Christ. . . . He had a vision of our Lady, too, under a similar form, without distinction of members. These visions confirmed him then in his faith and have always confirmed him so strongly that he often thought that if there were no scriptures to teach us those truths, he would be ready to die for them solely on the strength of what he then saw." His biographers pay much attention to his spiritual experience on one occasion by the river Cardoner, near the cave at Manresa where he had done penance and had been tempted even to the point of suicide. Ignatius himself writes of that moment: "It is impossible to set out in detail all that he then understood, and the most he can say is that he received so great an enlightenment of mind that, taking together all the things he has learned and known during the whole course of his life up to the age of 62 years now passed, he does not think they amount to as much as he received from that one illumination. It left him with an understanding so greatly enlightened that he seemed to himself to be another man, with another mind than that which was his before."

Ignatius was, then, a mystic, a charismatic Christian raised up by God at a crucial period of the Church's history. Like other charismatic figures, he attracted both the devotion and the suspicions of men. He made disciples, both men and women, but he was also examined by the Inquisition and put in jail, on suspicion of being one of the *alumbrados.*

But mysticism was only one side of this remarkable man and of his experience of prayer. The other side was his pragmatism, as it has been called, his *discretio* (to use that beautiful word which he liked to use, and which he had inherited from the Benedictine tradition), his sense of the Church. Hugo Rahner has suggested that the genuine mysticism which we see in Ignatius as in the other great Christian and Catholic saints can be summed up in the phrase: *caritas discreta,* a discreet charity. This blend of the inner flame, the inner vision, with a certain realism, with a sense of the Church, with a willingness to submit the inner vision to the hierarchical Church, with all her sins and ugliness, this difficult tension between charism and institution, this being simultaneously a man of the kingdom and a man of the Church, is what characterizes in a special way the personality and spirituality of Ignatius of Loyola. Incidentally, it is in the refusal to flee either to *enthusiasm,* i.e. to an elitist and separatist Christianity, or to an institutionalism which quenches the inner flame, that Rosemary Haughton, in her recent book, *Act of Love,* sees the authentic and integral verification of Christian faith.

This pragmatic mystic, Ignatius, did what other mystics had done before him—he shared his vision with the Church. Benedict had done it in a rule; Francis of Assisi had done it with his Canticle. A little later Teresa of Avila and John of the Cross were to do it in their own way. Ignatius did it in a very distinctive way. He began to share his experience of prayer with others, men and women, and as he did so over a few decades, he began to make notes about these "exercises." Between 1522, the year after his conversion, and 1548, these notes developed into what we now know as the *Spiritual Exercises* of St. Ignatius Loyola.

As I have said, they are not a book to be read. They are a

teacher's manual, so to speak. Like most manuals they are, as a text, rather dull, prosaic, uninspiring. But the remarkable thing is that this assortment of meditations and directives, in the hands of men like Ignatius himself, was one of the most powerful instruments of conversion and renewal in the post-Tridentine Church. Let us look a little at these *Exercises*, and first at what is most obvious, and least devotional, the decisional side, the concern for a good decision or election, as Ignatius calls it. There is, first of all, the title, which, by the way, doesn't come at the beginning (n. 21). Before the title there are twenty annotations, or introductory observations, which provide ground rules for the director of an Ignatian retreat. They tell him, for example, not to talk too much, not to get between the retreatant and the Holy Spirit, what to do when the retreatant is experiencing peace and consolation, and what to do when he is in trouble and desolation, how to adapt the *Exercises* to people who are too busy to make all thirty days at once, or people who are not really capable of such a major effort at conversion. It is all very hard-headed, very pragmatic, full of purpose.

Then there is the famous Principle and Foundation, which is not so much points for a meditation as a basic context and presupposition for all the meditations and contemplations. Here again we see the pragmatic Ignatius concerned with ends and means. Man was created for a purpose. Everything else is to help him achieve that purpose. He must use things only to achieve his purpose. He must be detached or indifferent so as to be able to use them in this way. The whole thing breathes logic rather than affection. God is mentioned just once, and Christ not at all.

If you keep turning the pages of the *Exercises*, you keep coming across pedestrian, dull, lifeless directives. A daily particular examination of conscience, complete with a chart for marking daily and weekly progress; a general examination of conscience, organized, as you might expect, according to thoughts, words and deeds.

Then there are the handy hints for prayer: before each Exercise a preparatory prayer and two or three preludes, techniques for recollection and reverence. There are the so-called additions, which suggest various ways of preserving recollection outside of the time of formal prayer as well as within it. This is where the remarks about keeping the shutters and doors closed to exclude light occur. There are some very sober remarks about penance.

Then, especially as the retreatant gets into the so-called Second Week of Exercises, there are a series of meditations and directives which are all aimed at paving the way for a good decision or election: "Introduction to Making a Choice of a Way of Life," "Matters About Which a Choice Should Be Made," "Two Ways of Making a Good and Correct Choice of a Way of Life" (the first contains six points; the second contains four rules and a note). In a way, it all reminds you of an article in *Reader's Digest*.

Then there are the rules: rules with regard to eating; rules for the discernment of spirits, some for the first week, some for the second; rules for the distribution of alms; some notes concerning scruples (who wouldn't be scrupulous, some might say, after all this paraphernalia?); and rules for thinking with the Church (where the famous remark occurs: "What seems to me white, I will believe black if the hierarchical Church so defines").

Such, then, are the *Spiritual Exercises* of St. Ignatius Loyola, a set of ground rules for someone who is making an important religious decision (or rather for the person directing him), so that he will make it according to God's will, not according to the evil spirit or his own selfishness. It is all geared to purposeful decision, to discernment of what God's will here and now is; it breathes an air of practicality, prudence. It is a crystallization of one very important aspect of the Ignatian experience and of the Ignatian way in prayer. It is prayer ordered to practical action and service.

But if this were all that the *Spiritual Exercises* were, it is

inconceivable that they could have had the impact on the life
of the Church for four centuries which in fact they have had,
that they could have been the soil on which Francis Xavier
and Peter Claver and Teilhard de Chardin grew to manhood
in Christ. If this were all that Ignatius was, it is inconceivable
that he would be the charismatic leader that he was and still,
in a way, is. Besides Ignatius the pragmatic, prudent man, the
man of purposeful decision, there was Ignatius the mystic,
the man who knew how to sing and dance, the man for whom
familiarity with God in prayer was the air he breathed. And,
in his *Spiritual Exercises*, the art form in which his life with
God in Christ is recorded, besides the practical directives and
rules and preludes, there are the contemplations of the life—
or rather of the mysteries of the life of Christ our Lord. In
a thirty-day retreat, by far the major part of the retreatant's
time in prayer is to be spent in these contemplations. He is
to take the text of Holy Scripture, approaching it with a loving
and reverent heart, aware of God's presence. He is to identify
with the mystery which is presented in the text—the Incarnation, the Annunciation, the Nativity, the Transfiguration, the
passion and death and resurrection. He is to identify with it
so much that, so far as possible, he puts himself in the scene,
sees the persons, listens to their words, observes what they
are doing. He is to be involved in the mystery, not as a mere
spectator, but as one who loves. For example, in the contemplation on the mystery of the birth of Jesus, "This will consist in seeing the persons, namely, our Lady, St. Joseph, the
maid, and the Child Jesus after his birth. I will make myself a
poor little unworthy slave, and as though present, look upon
them, contemplate them, and serve them in their needs with
all possible homage and reverence." This kind of involvement
will naturally lead to loving dialogue. In the contemplation on
the Incarnation: "I will think over what I ought to say to the
three divine persons, or to the eternal Word incarnate, or to
his mother, our Lady. According to the light I have received,

I will beg for grace to follow and imitate more closely our Lord, who has just become man for me." Note that "who has *just* become man for me." What is going on here is not just remembering an historical event. It is the reenacting of the mystery itself, here and now, as I pray. Here and now, as I pray, the Word is made flesh again, Jesus is born again, he preaches, he heals, he suffers, he rises again—and I am identified with him in my loving contemplation of these mysteries.

What matters here is not the particular imaginative form of the contemplation—many different forms are possible. What matters is that here, as the predominant prayer of the *Spiritual Exercises*, is a prayer that is not decisional but contemplative, not purposeful, but meaningful, not concerned, not pragmatic, but the prayer of presence, the prayer of simple identification with Christ in his mysteries.

I cannot pretend to speak as an expert on the *Spiritual Exercises* of St. Ignatius, except in the sense that someone who has tried to make them each year for thirty years and who has made them twice for thirty days can be an expert. But I am convinced that their extraordinary power comes in large part from the fact that they are a remarkable blend of contemplative and decisional prayer, of meaning and purpose, of mystery and problem.

Whenever you have an extraordinary document like this, you can be sure that the experts will have differences about interpreting it. Now one of the major points of disagreement among scholars is whether the *Exercises* are aimed predominantly at decision ("election"), or whether they are predominantly a school of contemplative prayer, an environment for bringing a person to complete docility to the Spirit in his life outside of retreat. I am not so foolhardy as to try to settle that quarrel. I am inclined to think that Ignatius himself thought of his *Exercises* predominantly as an instrument of conversion, a medium of radical decision in the life of a Christian, especially of someone with a large potential for apostolic dedication. But I am also inclined to think that he himself was not too concerned with the duality of contemplation and decision, meaning and purpose. He was, in his *Exercises*, more artist and artisan than scientist or technician. He had experienced himself how the two came together, and he had the ability to share this experience with others in a retreat situation. His was not the charism of the theoretician of Christian conversion and Christian spirituality, but the charism of sharing with others the lived experience.

One last word about Ignatius and his *Exercises* before I turn to contemplative and decisional prayer in our own lives. Part of his genius, I think, was his realization that a good decision or election was not merely one justified in rational and objective terms, but one in which the person or subject of decision was in the best possible attitude, primarily in terms of availability for the promptings of the Spirit. Ignatius doesn't talk too much in his meditations about the Holy Spirit. The last mystery is the Ascension; he doesn't go on to Pentecost. But perhaps, we may say, this is because the retreat itself is Pentecost, or rather the waiting in the upper room for the Spirit to come at Pentecost. I said before that Ignatius had an incredible ability to wait, not to act until it was clear that the action was from the Spirit. But this waiting was not a sterile doing of nothing. It was to be spent in loving contemplation of the mysteries, so that when the moment for decision came, the decider, the discerner, would be a man completely open to the Spirit of Christ, because he had been loving Christ in his mysteries constantly. As the Marxist Ernst Bloch has pointed out, before you can have great projects and plans, you must first dream dreams. Humanity owes much to its great engineers and planners and builders, but it owes much more to its dreamers, its contemplatives, its mystics. This is true of humanity as a whole, and it is true of each individual in the project of his life. Ignatius saw this, in a nontheoretical way, and he provided in his *Spiritual Exercises* a way—one way, let me add, a way that is not for all, and a way that must not be absolutized for anyone—in which contemplation and decision, our dreams and our projects, could come together in an integral life of prayer.

Let me say again that I am not at all interested in selling the *Spiritual Exercises* to anyone. I am putting forward the simple thesis that an integral life of prayer for any Christian is going to include contemplation and decision, and must succeed somehow in incarnating contemplation in decision, and making decision in turn minister to further contemplation. I am affirming, therefore, a certain necessary duality in the Christian life. I am aware that there are many today who are impatient with duality, and nervous when people begin to make this kind of distinction. I am perfectly willing to acknowledge that the perfection of human life, when we enter into the kingdom, will no longer contain this duality, for we will no longer have to create ourselves, or let the Spirit create us, through conversion, decision, option. Even in this life, I am willing to admit, there is possible a growth by which the duality of contemplation and decision is gradually transcended. I would think that the Ignatian formula (a phrase used not by Ignatius but about him by one of his first disciples), *in actione contemplativus*, contemplative in action, and that other formula used by Ignatius himself, "finding God in all things," point to this ideal of growing integration of contemplation and action, contemplation and decision. But for us who are still pilgrims (and Ignatius himself in his autobiography referred to himself in the third person as simply: the Pilgrim), this duality is a fact of life which we will ignore only to our own loss.

It is a fact of life which can be studied in its psychological, as well as in its theological and ascetical dimension. The rich and mature human personality, it seems to me, is a person in whom play and toil, leisure and work, contemplation and action, meaning and purpose, living in depth and decision, experience and judgment, are present and integrated in an harmonious whole. There will be, in humanity and in the Church, a rich variety of blends of these two characteristics of personhood. The call of each person as well as of particular communities of persons can be viewed, perhaps, from this point of view. Some of us are called to be predominantly the decision-makers, the framers of laws, the men of power and influence in this pragmatic sense. Others are called to be the music-makers, the dreamers of dreams (who, if I remember and interpret the poet correctly, are the real world-shakers by the very fact of their world-forsaking). We might appreciate the variety of forms of religious life in the Church from this point of view. But no one of us can be truly human unless we are capable of both. And our life of prayer, which is to say, our life of faith, living humanly and Christianly from our faith and hope in Christ, will prosper to the degree to which we are able to keep both alive and related in a fruitful complementarity and tension.

Another very attractive way of putting what I have been trying to say is the way employed by Fr. Fred Crowe, S.J., in three articles, "Complacency and Concern in the Thought of St. Thomas," in *Theological Studies* (20 [1959] 1-39; 198-230; 343-395), and less technically, in *Cross and Crown*. His basic thesis is that, for St. Thomas and in fact, the reality of love contains a certain duality, which he expresses in the terms, complacency and concern. Theologians have tended to conceive of love, whether it is self-centered love or altruistic love, as movement toward a good or toward a beloved. Fr. Crowe suggests that, before it is a principle of movement, of tendency, intention, appetite, concern, love is itelf a term, a receptivity, a *complacentia* (a being-pleased-with), a simple acquiescence and presence. He tries to show some points of contact between this duality and some modern and contemporary currents of thought, especially in Schopenhauer, Nietzsche and existentialists like Heidegger. Permit me to quote his summary of the contribution he thinks his distinction of complacency and concern can make:

> To the endless striving of Schopenhauer's will one opposes a will that has the double function of striving and resting; and this resting will not be an ennui that lacks an object for which to strive but, at least when willing is subordinated to contemplation, a joy complementary to an intellect that is fully occupied with its object. To Nietzsche's dissatisfaction with being and preoccupation with becoming, one opposes a will that regards being peacefully, to his active "will be" [one opposes] a passive "is"; and by the same stroke one settles the basic laws of right and wrong that regulate efforts to become. To a human existence whose structure is simply defined by care, one opposes not only the hope that modifies care from within, but a complacency that offsets care from without and reduces it to a subordinate rank below a prior correspondence with being. The mature philosopher and theologian equipped with a balanced view of man and the universe recovers the natural and spontaneously joyful orientation to being that the child originally had and lost in the desert of his concerns. (TS 20 [1959] 371 f.)

Interestingly enough, and in a very perceptive way, Fr. Crowe relates his complacency-concern dyad to the *Spiritual Exercises* of Ignatius, which, he says:

> recognize throughout the unpredictable nature of grace and await its guidance while disposing the exercitant to respond. That is, there is a permanent passive element in the life ruled by the Holy Spirit, and the *Exercises* respect it. Secondly, even the very active effort of the decision (the Ignatian election) supposes a *velle absolute* which we have linked closely with complacency . . . Again, the

General Examen of the same manual, though it has to do with personal sins, begins with thanksgiving and only afterwards turns to self-accusation and purpose of amendment. But thanksgiving is properly the act of those who have been passive, who have received without doing; it presupposes what is and the will's complacency in what is. And this complacency precedes the *intentio boni* of amendment in the Ignatian prayer." (*Ibid.* 374)

This last remark, I think, on gratitude for what *is*, preceding the purpose of amendment, touches on the heart of the Gospel. Before there is the Christian imperative, the exhortation to conversion and change, there must come first the Christian indicative, the celebration of the change which God in Christ has already wrought in human life. Before there is struggling, hopeful concern and purposeful action into the future, there must be grateful memory of the mighty deed of God our Father in raising Jesus from the dead, there must be recollection of the gift of the Spirit and the love of God for us poured forth in our hearts. Before we go forth in peace to love and serve the Lord, we must first celebrate the Lord's love for us. Before we do, we must be. Before we function, we must exist. Before we play a role, we must be a person. Before there is purpose in our lives, there must be meaning. Before love can give, it must first receive. Before we breathe forth love on the world, we must breathe in the Spirit of God.

There are many ways of saying the same thing, or perhaps of saying several things just a little different from one another, but all very close to the one thing that can never really be said. Dan Berrigan said it in that happy saying: "Don't just do something (said Buddha); *stand there.*" And Jesus, in the traditional interpretation, said it when he replied, "Martha, Martha, you worry and fret—you are concerned—about so many things; and yet few are needed, indeed only one. It is

Mary who has chosen the better part; it is not to be taken from her" (Lk 10:41).

Just a few years ago I would have hesitated a long time before quoting that familiar line to American religious. I might have sounded a little bit too much like a Roman cardinal struggling in vain to get the veils back on the sisters, and the sisters safely back inside the cloister walls. But these past few years have taught us a few things: we are a little embarrassed now, as we read the *Feast of Fools,* when we recall the things we thought and said a few years ago after we had read *The Secular City.* I fully realize that, even today, a call to contemplation can bring a false comfort and consolation to individuals and groups for whom "contemplation" means prayers and not prayer, a refuge against faith, not a plunge into faith. But, despite the risk, we must affirm being, meaning, complacency, the better part. If there is any hazard in renewal among American religious at this present juncture, I would suggest that it is the danger of being too much like Avis, of trying too hard, of being, like Martha, too concerned. There is a time for everything under heaven—so says the wise man and the song. And the time has come for breathing, for the first moment of love which is a moment not of movement but of expectancy, waiting, complacency.

Finally, if we need any further incentive for righting the balance of complacency and concern, we need only look at the crisis in our society today. Are we not spectators—involved spectators—at a progressive alienation between two worlds: the world of science and technology, of pragmatic, purposeful concern, of decision-making process, of the mastery of life, dominion over the earth and the universe, of *homo faber,* man the maker; and, on the other side, the world of unconcern, the world of the cop-out, of the flower-people, of mystical fads, and drug trips, the world of Woodstock, of complacency. Isn't there a real value present in each of these worlds?

And isn't the tragedy precisely in the estrangement between the two, which need each other and complement each other? And finally, if religious men and women, through our experience of prayer and faith and charity, attain by God's grace to a certain relative wholeness and reconciliation of complacency and concern, isn't there something we can say to our contemporary world?

13

PROSPECTUS:
RELIGIOUS LIFE AS COUNTERCULTURAL

Having heeded the call of Christian secularity, inviting them to "get with it," religious now seem called to "get against it," and to assume, with the whole Church, a more critical stance toward contemporary culture and society.

The most beautiful introduction to a theological talk I have ever heard consisted of just four words: *The Gospel is wonderful.* The Gospel is indeed wonderful. Jesus Christ, who is proclaimed in the Gospel, who is the Gospel, is simply wonderful. The Gospel is wonderful and it creates wonder in us. It is wonderful because it is inexhaustible. To believers of every age, every culture, every mentality, it speaks with power and inspiration. It is rich in its variety, yet penetrating in its singlemindedness. In every age it goes right to the heart of the human problem, because it comes from him who is the heart of the world, Jesus Christ, our crucified and risen Lord.

The wonderfulness of the Gospel is being exhibited at the moment that I write in the dramatic change of perspective and accent to which it now calls Christians. Ten, even five, years ago, the name of the game was "Christian secularity."

Today it is: *counterculture, apocalyptic*. Then we were summoned, quite legitimately, to get with it; now the call is to stand against it.

In bringing this group of reflections on the religious life to a close, and in noting, without melancholy, how provisional all such reflections must be, let me sketch how I see the developments of the past decade or so, and suggest what might be the perspective of an historian in 1984 (standing perhaps on a broken arch of the George Washington bridge) as he looks back on the sixties and seventies. In doing this I wish to advance the twofold thesis that the Church is being called to a critical, countercultural stance toward contemporary American society and culture, and that religious have a crucial role in shaping and expressing this stance.

Until the last decade or so, Roman Catholics of the United States were much preoccupied with proving to themselves and to others that they were, despite their Roman Catholicism, good Americans. As a largely immigrant Church, Continental and Irish, we had to make our way in, and into, the so-called "Wasp" culture. This was a long and painful struggle, but somewhere in the thirties, forties, fifties, we seemed to have made it. The election to the presidency of John F. Kennedy was a landmark and symbol. But even as that transition from being aliens and strangers was being concluded, another more subtle and difficult struggle began to be seen in clearer perspective. From about the time of World War II, we began to see that Roman Catholics were immigrants not just geographically and in respect of American culture but in the modern world as a whole. That world, shaped by the Reformation, the French and American revolutions, the Enlightenment, by the scientific, industrial, technological, and communication revolutions, that world of Darwin and Marx, Freud and Einstein, was a world which had come into being mostly without the Church, against the Church, and with opposition from the Church. The Syllabus of Errors of Pius IX and the anti-

Modernist pronouncements under Pius X became symbolic of the negative and embattled stance of Roman Catholicism in a world not of its making.

Gradually, however, from the time of Pope Leo XIII, this situation of being cultural immigrants in the modern world began to change. One perspective on Pope John XXIII and Vatican II may be expressed by saying that, with them, Roman Catholicism came to terms with modernity. The decade or so since Vatican II has witnessed a strong preoccupation with being men and women of our own age, despite our Catholicism, and even despite our Christianity. Leslie Dewart's book, *The Future of Belief,* posed the problem very precisely: How can one be a believing Christian and a contemporary man? In a more popular and spectacular way, Harvey Cox's *The Secular City* became a kind of Bible of Christian accommodation. Contemporary man was judged to be inexorably scientific, technological, pragmatic, secular. Religious myth and sacred symbol had lost their hold on him. If Christianity were to speak effectively to him, it had to relinquish its traditional aura of sacredness and mystery, had to come into the marketplace, had to exhibit Jesus as the Man for Others, had to join in the secular struggle for justice and peace. A quite different current, stemming from the writings of Teilhard de Chardin, had this in common with the influence from writers like Dewart and Cox, Bonhoeffer and Bishop Robinson, that it called Christians to identify with the culture around them, whatever the risk.

In response to this call, many religious in the American Church accepted a certain secularization of life and mentality, expressed in dress, life style, choice of ministries. We just had to be "with it." We had to prove to ourselves and to others that Christians and religious could be contemporary men and women, that the Gospel and the life of the counsels were not fatally wedded to a sacral or medieval or Greco-Roman or even Semitic culture.

And then—the Gospel is wonderful! Precisely at the moment when we began to feel ready to come to terms with the contemporary world, when our theology, our spirituality, our liturgy were in process of rapid and extensive change so that we could be comfortable in the modern world, along came the Spirit to disturb us once again. For now it becomes clear that this culture, this contemporary American and Western society into which we were at such pains to enter, was a demonic and dying one, or at least an ambivalent one. In the last several years we have come to experience that science, technology and communications do not solve our basic problems of human living, and in fact can compound them in a terrifying way. They can confirm us in our inhumanity. Confronted with the apparently insoluble problems of our society, war, poverty, injustice, the destruction of the material environment, the destruction of persons through an inhuman work milieu, appalled by the general dehumanization of life, we are having second thoughts about whether we need or want to identify with such a culture.

Within the past few years, the cutting edge of theology and spirituality has begun to shift from an accommodative to a resistant stance. Before speaking of how this shift may affect our understanding and living of the religious life, it might be well to illustrate this movement briefly from recent theological reflections.

First, there is an older work which is not so much an instance of the new accent as a helpful background for interpreting. It is the little essay of H. Richard Niebuhr, *Christ and Culture*.[1] It shows how in the course of Christian history various facets of the Gospel, as embodied in great thinkers and charismatic leaders, were brought to bear on the relationship of the Church and the surrounding culture. The very titles of the chapters of this work point to an historical pluralism of posture: Christ Against Culture; Christ Above Culture; Christ

[1] H. Richard Niebuhr, *Christ and Culture* (Harper & Row).

Within Culture; Christ Transforming Culture. What is today characterized as apocalyptic or countercultural is, therefore, not without precedent in Christian history, even though it has not always been dominant.

Secondly, the "theology of liberation," especially in its Latin American interpretation by such authors as Gustavo Guttierez and Rubem Alves, presents to American Roman Catholics an embarrassing challenge to their acquiescence in the political, economic and cultural status quo.[2] In the context of the growing gap between rich and poor nations, the theology of liberation offers a strong criticism of the idea and praxis of development, even as this is broadly and humanistically understood (as, for example, in the Encyclical of Pope Paul, "On the Development of Peoples"). It offers as alternative the theological notion of liberation (etymologically, "redemption" is linked with "liberation") as pivotal, and analyzes our present situation as calling for self-liberation by the oppressed through struggle against tyrannical structures and dehumanizing cultural forces. This struggle works especially through an educational process, in which human communities are formed through critical reflection wedded to militant action (consciencization).[3]

Thirdly, the "political theology" of Johannes Metz contains a call to the Church to be critical of the prevailing status quo. By "deprivatizing" theology and asceticism, and by calling for a "militant eschatology" which submits society today to a searching critique from the standpoint of man's future, Metz too is calling for a radical faith which refuses to come to terms with reigning ideologies.[4]

Fourthly, a plausible basis for the current critique of "sinful structures" is afforded by Piet Schoonenberg's analysis of

[2] G. Guttierez, *A Theology of Liberation* (Orbis, 1973); R. Alves, *A Theology of Human Hope* (Corpus, 1968).
[3] See P. Freire, *Pedagogy of the Oppressed*.
[4] J. Metz, *Theology of the World* (Herder and Herder, 1969).

the traditional concept of original sin in terms of "the sin of the world," understanding this not as an inherited guilt but as the radical vitiation of the moral environment of man through the accumulation of human sins.[5] This perspective is enlarged by similar reflections of Karl Rahner on the notion of concupiscence, which has traditionally been understood as sinful inclinations or inner disorder within man. Rahner suggests that we attend to the socialization of concupiscence which takes place when man's sinfulness is projected into his social processes, structures and institutions.[6] The implication of this concept for the ascetical struggle is that it be directed simultaneously to the conquest of personal selfishness and to the conquest of institutionalized evil in society and culture. The result is an integration of the personal and the social, the private and the public, traditional asceticism and the new struggle of the Church for peace and justice in the world.

Fifthly, a similar effort, by James Douglass in *Resistance and Contemplation*, views the integration of the twofold struggle with the help of a Yin-Yang notion. Only he who contemplates really seeks the liberation of man; only he who is somehow engaged in the struggle for peace and justice really contemplates.[7]

Finally, a little work which situates the present trend of counter-cultural Christianity within a biblical perspective is the paperback of Carl Braaten, *Christ and Counter-Christ*, where the category of "apocalyptic" is brought to bear on the need to struggle with the darknesses of contemporary Western culture.[8]

If one accepts this first thesis, then, that the Church is

[5] P. Schoonenberg, *Man and Sin* (University of Notre Dame Press, 1965).

[6] K. Rahner in: *Theology for Renewal* (ed. L. Shook; Sheed and Ward, 1964).

[7] J. Douglass, *Resistance and Contemplation* (Doubleday, 1972).

[8] C. Braaten, *Christ and Counter-Christ* (Fortress, 1972).

being called in the name of the Gospel to a critical stance toward the cultural and societal status quo, what are the implications for the life of religious? The primary fact for shaping our response to this question is that historically religious life has been a special critical, counter-cultural, apocalyptic agency in the life of the Church and of mankind. Here it might be well to recall what was said in a previous essay on celibacy as a challenge to tribalism. The claim there made may be broadened to include the other principal dimensions of religious life, poverty and obedience, contemplation and community, asceticism and apostolic witness. Besides being an exclamation point, a sign of the Good News that has come and is still coming, the life of monks and of other religious has traditionally been a question mark placed after all human engagements at the point at which these tend to become idolatrous and hence destructive of the human. From the fathers of the desert on, through a wide variety of forms but always with the same challenging implications, the life of the counsels has been given to the Church not only as a sign of divine mercy but as a sign of divine judgment.

It is here appropriate to recall the paradox exhibited in another brief essay in this book, by which some religious, at least, have functioned as civil servants in the Church while pursuing the radical and charismatic vocation of challenging the Church.

If this understanding of religious life is accepted, then what may we say of the role of religious in the coming decade, when the entire Church, it seems, will be called to protest and counter the inhumanity of much in contemporary culture and society?

First, let me state what religious are *not* being asked to do. They are not being asked to disavow the movement of several years ago into Christian secularity, nor to return to the mentality and style of pre-Vatican II days. The new accent on asceticism, unworldliness, eschatology, is sharply different from that which, legitimately, has been left behind. There had prevailed a tyranny of sacred forms which needed to be disavowed. In a sense, the movement of Christian secularity, while accommodative with respect to secular culture, was counter-cultural with respect to sacred culture. It had to disengage from that dying culture. It had to be present within the contemporary before it could legitimately counter the contemporary. There is no passage to adulthood except through adolescence. In the present call to be anti-worldly, there is no comfort for an antiquated or disembodied unworldliness. If certain apocalyptic values are now being reaffirmed, they are too powerful and heady for the old bottles of a post-Tridentine spirituality.

Next, religious are not being asked to identify their Christian faith with any particular counter-culture. Faith needs to find appropriate cultural—and counter-cultural—expression, but it must always be wary of a Babylonian captivity by any human construction. If the Gospel represents a powerful critique of cultural idolatry, it does so in a way which transcends the purely political, economic, social or cultural. Jesus refused to be diverted into a political partisan or secular judge. The Church is faithful to man as well as to God to the degree to which she points man toward the Absolute present within his life. Likewise, religious can be of service to the poor and oppressed only to the degree to which their loving engagement in the works of mercy and in the work of justice carries with it a new horizon of human aspiration not accessible through purely secular agencies, namely a human life lived according to the beatitudes.

If this is what is *not* being asked of religious, what *is* being asked? First, that they accept from God, who often speaks through unlikely messengers, a critique of *their own* lives and attitudes, precisely as they themselves have failed to carry out Paul's injunction not to be conformed to this world. It would be both arrogant and naive were religious to undertake a crusade against the dehumanizing forces of contemporary society without realizing how far they themselves presently compromise the Gospel message through consumerism, status-seeking, irreverence toward the material environment, and other culture-induced attitudes. Hence, criticism of the world and self-criticism must be conceived as two inseparable dimensions of the one ascetical effort.

Secondly, life within the Church as a whole must continue to be a target of critical reflection and conversion. Ecclesiastical culture, too, can be vitiated and can work against the human, both by succumbing to inhuman influences from secular culture and by creating its own vested interests and absolutized structures. When the poor are uncomfortable in the Church, when official Church organizations spend precious resources in luxury or mere display, when scrambling for position becomes characteristic of Churchmen, we are in the presence of decay, not of the new creation. One has only to recall how hard-fought and still incomplete has been the struggle for justice and respect for the person within the Church to appreciate how much the Church herself needs to procreate a salutary critique of herself.

But it would be misleading to accent excessively this negative aspect of the call to a countercultural stance. To be critical and countercultural involves affirmation and creativity as well as negation and disengagement. The most important dimension of what we are here describing, perhaps, is the call to verify new modes of life and action alternative to those which we are rejecting. Religious are given by God and by the rest of the Church the gift of a certain leisure not enjoyed by many others precisely so that their life together can exhibit new possibilities of human life. Where else today should we be able to find, for example, a deeper reverence for the goods of the earth, a clearer sanity in attitudes and practices regarding bodily health and beauty, a more persevering effort to originate new patterns of work and leisure, and more adventuresome explorations into the life of contemplation? If religious are not free enough to develop alternatives to contemporary decadence touching every aspect of human living, who else can be expected to be free?

And finally, what religious choose to do with their material and personal resources in various forms of service is also a crucial area of nay-saying to contemporary culture and of yea-saying to Christ and to Gospel values. Not only what we choose but how we choose reveals the degree of our humanness and of our Christian faith. In a world of status seekers and social climbers, where the haves get more and the have-nots lose the little they have, what kind of apostolic investment do religious wish to make? Will they be content to service schools, for example, where no real challenge is addressed to students, parents or faculty to call into question prevailing assumptions about human values? In social and medical ministries will they acquiesce in an apostolic drift which leaves them mere functionaries in a system wedded to the welfare of the comfortable while the poor are abandoned to inferior status? What a beautiful day has dawned in a religious community when it finds itself truly free to disengage from caretaker tasks in a decrepit society and to devote itself instead to action which prepares a better tomorrow for man, especially for the poor.

Here then, as it seems to me, is where the call of the next decade lies for religious—a return to the tradition of innovative challenge, and a corresponding disengagement from the tired and sick modes of life and action now imposed upon us by contemporary culture. The current renascence of apocalyptic in the consciousness of the Church, while it brings back a salutary awareness that there is no victory without combat, and no liberation without shedding of blood, is restoring even more the sense of new life, a new creation.

"Then the One sitting on the throne spoke: 'Now I am making the whole of creation new'" (Rev 21:5). By no special merit but as pure gift, religious in the Church today are privileged to share in this thrilling call to proclaim and embody in their life and ministry the fact that, with Jesus Christ, the whole of creation is renewed, and the world of the past is gone.